How We Watch Sports

How We Watch Sports

The Evolution of Fandom and Sports
Consumption in the #postinternet Era

DAN VOICESCU

ISBN-13: 9781532727832
ISBN-10: 1532727836
Library of Congress Control Number: 2016906141
CreateSpace Independent Publishing Platform
North Charleston, South Carolina

Foreword

WELCOME TO THE Show!

My initial intent was to entitle the book How *To* Watch Sports, but the risk of sounding pompous and sanctimonious was too much to bear. A procedural guide about the mechanics and logistics of sports-watching was not something I was interested in.

After spending weeks debating whether to pose a question in the title or not, I decided against it. The question would be too loaded. Fans and readers alike would be demanding concrete answers. Instead, I set out to give an overview of the wide emotional spectrum that the post-internet sports ecosystem has created. I use "post-internet" to describe the modern state of social interaction and media consumption during the current times of widespread internet adoption. Social and digital media, two formidable instruments, have joined forces to shake up traditional sports fandom, providing us with the type of sports consumption experience that would have seemed unfathomable in the pre-internet era (i.e. a short twenty years ago).

How We Watch Sports - all the drama, emotions, tweets, texts, memes, gifs, vines, gambling, fantasy, socializing, #nextlevel distractions and disruptions around the act of sports consumption. The omnipresence of social media, the anachronism of the traditional, stereotypical sports fan. These are the things that have fascinated me, things that everyone has been talking about in snippets, using catchy buzzwords and adages, but without really scratching deeper under the surface to try and reveal how technological progress has altered our mentality as sports fans at large.

My hope is that the following pages comprise an entertaining journey through the intricate maze of contemporary fandom, as well as give you a small window into the soul of the modern, well-connected fan. The technology around us keeps changing at breakneck speed, so I kindly ask for your indulgence as you navigate through these pages. The collective fan mentality shifts and evolves along, as we, modern sports fans at large, try to keep up and make sense of it all.

Enjoy the Game!

Danny V.

How We Watch Sports

The Highest of Emotional Highs, Worlds Apart

April 16, 1986

O VERCAST EASTERN EUROPEAN spring afternoon, cheap contraband cigarette smoke choking this young scribe's lungs. Army soldiers in green tunics filling the stadium section located right under the scoreboard, location that would eventually become the Ultras section. A few sections over, three generations of Romanian soccer fanatics gathered to witness live and in person a Champions Cup[1] semifinal. An once-in-a-lifetime experience across all three age groups.

Sitting down, barely able to see anything, kicking sunflower seeds and listening to the banter and the disjointed battle cries (*On them, on their mama...*) hours before the game, an affair that would come to define what it is to love sports, and would set a reference point for peak fandom ecstasy. In much the same way that the emotional highs of a first love or sexual encounter cannot be replicated, neither can the feeling you get watching your childhood idols perform at the highest level, entertaining and dominating in front of yours truly's impressionable nine-year-old eyes. It was all happening. The show, the drama, a culmination of months of anticipation and speculation. All the built-up tension and emotion finally released live within the confines of a stuffy concrete bowl. There was no better feeling than this.

---

1 Precursor to the modern day Champions League, the premier club soccer competition in the world.

November 30, 2013

Sipping on East African medium roast, laid out in a cozy northern Virginia basement, sounds of "Uncle Verne" Lundquist permeating the muted silence strictly enforced during my two-month-old's first Iron Bowl nap. And quite a memorable nap that turned out to be, although less so for him than for his ol' man. iPhone in hand, toggling between texting, social media, and real-time gambling odds, twenty-seven years and an entire world removed from that glorious Bucharest spring in 1986, yet still yearning for that magical feeling of ecstasy by association. An entirely different experience, consumed across a different continent, sport, demographic and a polar opposite comfort level. After three plus hours of drama, and as Chris Davis' "kick six" return crossed the end zone, I ended up in the same emotional place as a quarter century prior – peak ecstasy, peak fandom. Bets were won, money was made, social media banter ensued, countless *I told you so's* dished out liberally … this time the fandom experience was more complicated and multi-layered. And yet, the same emotional peak. On top of the world, baby.

Beyond the previously unimaginable technological advances and dramatic changes to the fandom scenery that came about during the last quarter century, the emotional aspects have stayed constant. The need to fully give yourself up to the sporting spectacle remains a quintessential part of the fandom experience, whether that spectacle happens to play out in an Eastern European concrete amphitheater or a Mid-Atlantic suburban basement in front of a high-definition screen (accompanied by another smaller screen), connecting you to the world and providing access to an unimaginable wealth of information. Despite circumstances that could not be more different from a generation prior, fans continue to share the same primal emotion— a need *to belong*, to be a part of a human bonding force transcending geography, demographics, and historical eras.

I don't know how *you* watch sports and I am not about to pass judgment on your fandom ways. Whatever your ritual happens to be; it is probably the fruit of a rigorous process. Much like sex[2], there is no *correct* way to be a fan.

Also just like sex, the more actively involved you are in sports watching, the better you become at it. I have no doubt that the countless hours, days, and years spent watching sports have made us savvier fans, better suited to relish the show. On the flip side, it is entirely possible that all that time spent consuming sports may have had a negative impact on our prowess and ability as sexual partners. Something has got to give...

The passion and engagement that we experience while watching sports are more intense and genuine than all other forms of entertainment or media content. You can't fake fandom and all its accompanying thrills or letdowns just like you can't fake love.

Pumping your fists and yelling like a man possessed while seeing *Hamilton*? Nope. No spectacle other than sports incites a more unbridled level of emotion.

The ability to derive pleasure from the act of watching a sporting event is a distinctive and personal experience, a judgment-free zone where everyone is free to bring in his or her own biases and baggage. The social experience of rooting for a team allows for flaws in judgment and logic, as long as our hearts are in the right place, and the same color fabric and team logo is threaded around us. You can't be a bad sports "lover" as long as your commitment and emotional rooting interest is sincere. Well, try that line of thinking in other realms, like the complicated (and unsportsmanlike) world of dating and relationships. Sincerity and strong feelings? That's not nearly enough to build a relationship. Things tend to get a lot more unwieldy there, man.

---

2 Please forgive the cheap analogy. I hope you're not prudish. Please don't be prudish. Also, sex sells and I need to pull all the tricks to get your attention. Lord knows there are actual games you could be watching instead...

We've come a Long Way, Baby

To GET A little perspective of our place in fandom history, let's take a quick walkabout through the history of sports coverage.

Budding Days of Sports Journalism and the Newspaper Era
The 856 BC wrestling match featuring two fellas by the names of Ajax and Odysseus marked the birth of sports coverage in written[3] form. None other than Homer wrote about the event, which ended in a draw, as Achilles, the referee, raised the arms of both contestants.

Fast-forward two and a half millennia and we find distinguished men of letters, such as Sir Arthur Conan Doyle of *Sherlock Holmes* fame, covering the 1908 London Olympics Marathon. Closer to home, the first instances of modern sports coverage in written form can be attributed to publications such as the *New York Post*, the *Charleston Courier* and the *Richmond Enquirer*, which all provided results of boxing matches in the early 1800s. The introduction and growing popularity of baseball in the 1850s brought about the first instances of team sports coverage in the *New York Herald* and *Spirit of the Times*. In the 1870s we see the first instances of sports sections. The 1890s, with the birth of basketball and football and the crowning of baseball as the national pastime, mark the genesis of modern

---

3 Handwritten form, to be precise—we are still some twenty-two centuries away from Gutenberg's printing press.

sports journalism. At the time sports coverage was largely limited to the box score, devoid of any context or descriptions.

Being a sports fan implied a tenuous relationship with the team you supported. Allegiances were born out of location and proximity. Considering transportation and general accessibility challenges, attending a live game meant being a part of a truly extraordinary event. Budding sports fans had to put their emotions on hold until the day after the game. Sleep on it, little fella. Before the radio era, the only ways of finding out the results were either through word of mouth or through the morning edition of the newspaper. Beyond the box score and the standings, there was very little detail available for the public discourse. Newspapers were not yet in the business of developing the athlete's cult of personality. Fan bases were defined along distinct geographical and regional lines. Very little in the form of nuanced content was available to the general public in the sports columns through the 1920s.

The 1930s represented the modern sports journalism boom, as newspapers began hiring sports editors to oversee content. Capitalizing on the larger-than-life sports personalities of the time (Babe Ruth, Jesse Owens, Max Baer) and the public's thirst for visual cues and imagery, newspapers began including in-depth profiles as well as cartoons as part of standard sports coverage. Cartoons became an integral part of the sports page, adding some context and in most cases stirring up emotions and controversies, two required elements in the creation process of the modern sports fan.

The Radio Era

Drawing us closer to the modern era, radio broadcasting changed the spectating game and introduced the era of live broadcasting to a national, *live* public audience on a grand scale. Many a parent and grandparent has regaled us with tales of listening to the ball game on radio and all the rewards and challenges associated with that experience. Such stories take us back to the early days of sports coverage, a time when fandom called on the hearing sense much more than the seeing sense. Being a fan implied more listening than actual *watching*. During the 1930s and 1940s, watching a live sporting event required live physical attendance in the stands. The transition from delayed, day after fandom to live, consume-it-as-it-happens events was significant and marked the turning point when sports, as a cultural phenomenon, became part of popular culture. The marquee events of the day were boxing matches and horse races. The 1921 boxing match featuring Jack Dempsey and Georges Carpentier finally brought the excitement of live sports into the homes of private citizens through radio broadcasting. The ability to plug in live and become a part of a popular phenomenon was now conceivable. Millions of new fans were introduced to athletes as role models and heroes through live commentary over radio waves.

It may seem boring and inconceivable today, but from the perspective of a 1921 boxing fan, tuning in to a radio wave frequency and immersing yourself in the words and the images depicted during the game was what finally made fandom possible. The announcers were given the vital task of creating a game-like atmosphere through words and intonation. Listening to a game was and still is a unique yet demanding experience, requiring an active presence and high level of engagement. With the help of the radio announcer, your mind's eye subconsciously creates a unique, personalized stadium setting and play-by-play action. While the general contours of this visualization are shared across the audience, the particular details of this internal visualization exercise are unique to each individual. Absent actual details, such as luminosity level, ambient noise level, and players' exact and actual location on the field or court, we are free to let our imaginations roam within the confines of the general descriptors laid out by the announcers. Our esteemed forefathers had the ability to imagine their own game, to draw up specific and personal details to complete and satisfy their spectating experience.

This activity requires a much higher level of engagement; it implies a higher attention level and minimizes the ability to multitask.

Sparing you all the *"Well, son, back in my day we ain't have no Internet machine and all these damn games on in high definition at all times of day,"* suffice to say that during my formative years as a sports fan, I was deprived of what is now accepted as the most basic form of sports coverage: live television broadcasting. Resorting to, and partaking in audio-only content presented through the airwaves was the norm. Having to tune in to the radio for two hours, clinging to the commentators' every word, analyzing the tone of voice, the highs and lows in commentary, in order to ascertain the level of danger to our goal or, better yet, to the opponent's goal is exactly the kind of thing that should make a budding fan swear off sports altogether, turning his attention to some instant gratification form instead. Consuming sports through radio prevented any sort of multitasking. By dividing your attention among different activities, you brought upon yourself the real risk of not sensing the flow of the game or worse - missing a key play. Worshipping at the altar of the radio became mandatory if you wanted to call yourself a fan.

Lest we forget what a consuming exercise this can be before harping on the benefits of putting your ear next to a transistor radio: In order to have been able to consume an actual game, to fully understand the proceedings occurring during the live action our predecessors engaged in a very disciplined yet exhausting ritual of listening. Here are some of the activities required during this type of sports consumption: full attention, general silence, no browsing of any sort, limited to no commentary or interaction with others during the game. This sounds awfully close to the experience of a believer in church during a three-hour sermon. It sounds exhausting and boring.

Far be it from me to claim that being a fan and generally following sports was a shitty experience back in the day. Not at all. It was, however, a *very* different exercise, requiring a higher level of commitment and imagination, an ability to visualize and play the game inside the mind's eye for an extended period of time. I can't imagine doing this in the present day. It seems so exhausting. We've swum out way too far in the crystal waters of HD and social media to ever dip our toes in that messy cesspool of radio.

About a year ago, I was stuck in traffic and missed the kickoff of a Giants game, so I turned on the radio and tuned in to the game. I was OK with the radio feed and the commentary initially. I didn't have another option anyway. But after about twenty minutes, once I was aware of the score and the general game action circumstances, I began finding the whole thing extremely boring and unrewarding. I shut off the radio, hit the gas pedal northbound on 10th Avenue, and decided that I had enough time to catch up with the live broadcast on DVR. *Fuhggetaboutit.* Spare me this audio-only play-by-play nonsense from my life.

The Television Era

*"Good afternoon, Ladies and Gentlemen. Welcome to the
first telecast of a sporting event. I'm not sure what it is we're
doing here, but I certainly hope it turns out well for you
people who are watching."*

(BILL STERN, 1939)

THE FIRST TELEVISED sporting event was a college baseball game
between Princeton and Columbia[4] in 1939. Let the irony not
be lost here—in the present modern era of live sports broadcasting
glut and overabundance, you'd be hard pressed to find a Columbia-
Princeton baseball game anywhere on your channel lineup or online.

*"Television got off the ground because of sports...Today,
maybe sports need television to survive, but it was just the
opposite when it first started. When we [NBC] put on the
World Series in 1947, heavyweight fights, the Army-Navy
football game, the sales of television sets just spurted."*

*(HARRY COYLE, DIRECTOR OF SPORTS PROGRAMMING, DUMONT
NETWORK AND NBC)*

---

4 Baker Field – the Birthplace of Sports Television!

The number of TV sets in use in jumped from a mere 190,000 in 1948 to 10 million in 1950. While this fifty-fold increase over only two years cannot be attributed exclusively to the rise of live sports broadcasting, it is worth highlighting that this 5,000 percent lift in the number of television sets coincides with the early boom of prime-time sports broadcasting on network television.

Mid-twentieth-century sports broadcasting was used mainly as a means to drive up the sales of television sets, with the overt approach of providing a public service to the masses by providing access and visual exposure to events that would be otherwise relegated to audio only. In the process, sport became Big Business. The networks captured the attention of tens of millions of eyeballs. The advertisers did not lag behind. The money followed. The public was now able to partake in the general excitement and to establish sporting culture as part of the thread that bonds local communities.

The early days of sports television were a simpler time, devoid of all the byzantine issues covered in today's countless media outlets. The audiences of the time were mainly just grateful to be able to be able to access live game footage from their homes. Along with the game footage on the screen, the accompanying voices became part of sports folklore. Game commentators became icons of the trade. Their voices, insights, and clichés became the foundation of the general perception of sport. Guys like Red Barber, Vin Scully, and Jack Buck were generally taken at face value. Without today's cacophony generated by myriad sports media outlets, these voices of the game were left unchallenged, respected, and accepted as gospel. Would these iconic commentators be able to thrive in today's sports media? Transcendent commentators such as Bob Murphy and Pat Summerall would have been subject to constant scrutiny. Any quirk or slip-up would give way to an instant Twitter roasting. Given a voice or a channel, haters are (always) gonna hate. Venom flows freely in today's post-internet age. Without the current army of talking heads coming after them, these titans of the industry were left largely to their own devices, able to develop unique styles and trademark expressions in unencumbered fashion.

The '60s and '70s were largely a black and white era, and not just when it came to the colors available on the TV screens. There were good guys and bad guys, winners and losers; the narrative was mostly of the "us versus them" variety; and you could either hit, shoot, and pass or you could not. You were either above the Mendoza line,[5] or you sucked. Absent second, third, or umpteenth opinions, the viewing public turned on the television sets for a simple pleasure. There was very limited nuance as part of the sports discourse in the early days of television. The fans of the day were just glad to partake in the simple pleasure of actually seeing game footage from the comfort of their living rooms.

High Definition
January 30, 2000: Kurt Warner's Nose Hairs on 720p Display
History repeats itself. Much like their savvy predecessors of the 40s and 50s, the turn of century television and broadcasters sales force realized that if they could offer a better sports viewing experience, sports fans were more likely to purchase the new high-definition television sets than the rest of the public who may be more into game shows or soap operas.

Y2K bug worries firmly behind, it was time to shift focus to the most watched event in American television history—the Super Bowl. Only this time, the public had the opportunity to observe this mega-event/game/spectacle in stunning high definition, bringing an incredible level of detail straight into their living rooms.

Super Bowl 34 (or XXXIV) marked the first time a major sports event was broadcast in HD (720p). At the time the full impact of high definition broadcasting was limited due to the low number of high definition television sets on the market. Nonetheless, sports

---

5 The "Mendoza Line" is used as common parlance in baseball, derived from the name of shortstop Mario Mendoza, whose mediocre batting average is taken to define the threshold of incompetent hitting.

consumption took off over the next decade, and much of the rise in ratings can be attributed to HD broadcasting as the driving force behind the proliferation and ubiquity of sports culture.

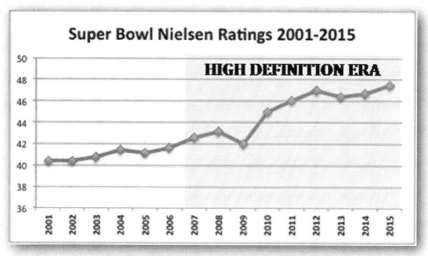

Nielsen TV rating is defined as the percentage of the US population aged 18–49 who watched a program.

Using Super Bowl ratings as a measure of increased sports consumption avoids muddying up the trend by excluding the popularity issue as a factor. NBA, MLB, and NHL playoff ratings are generally determined by the popularity or the market size of the teams involved in the finals or playoffs series. Super Bowl, being a one-game, one-time event, generally avoids that issue. Everyone tunes in. What's remarkable here is the significant difference in average annual ratings growth between the pre-HD and the HD years. Between 2001 and 2006 (the "pre-HD era"), this annualized rate was 0.62 percent. The comparable growth rate for years from 2006 to 2015 is a whopping 1.5 percent annually, or 1.4 times higher. This average rate does *not* exclude a significant one-time decrease in 2009 (-2.5 percent versus 2008). The ratings' stabilization at around 46 to 47 percent also coincides with the stabilization in the growth rate of HD TV sets on the market.

To take a small step back and put it all in perspective, a short eighty years ago, radio introduced the first elements of live sports consumption. Following radio, television brought into play another one of our five senses, presumably completing the process of bringing live sports into our homes. On a grand scale, enhancing the quality of the television broadcast may not register as a game changer; however, once at-home spectators were presented with a level of visual detail that rivaled the live stadium experience, the choice between seeing a game in person or watching from the comforts of our homes became a much more complicated one.

Super Bowl 36 (or XXXVI) marked the first sporting event I watched in high definition. The event was broadcast in subpar 720p (an unacceptable resolution by today's standards, causing many a millennial to roll their eyes). My HD cherry had popped. There was no going back to pixelated, standard definition content, and now I needed more of this awesome content. What will they think of next to enhance our fandom experience?[6]

Stay tuned.

---

6 Without spoiling the section of the book that deals with future technology, it turns out that what they are thinking of I terms of TV technology is bending the screen and cramming even more pixels in it, in order to make the image quality as close to real life as possible.

The Live Stadium Experience in the Modern Era

THE PRESENT DAY fan experience is a complicated and evolving relationship between fans, teams (or franchises, team owners and the leagues governing each sport, with the means of content delivery serving as the conduit. So far we have quickly surveyed the at-home experience. To add another significant ingredient into the current sports consumerist crockpot, we need to enter the modern stadium era, in which sports venues are increasingly digitized and transformed into plush settings set up for a sensory overload experience. Forced to keep up pace with the multilayered fandom experience offered in private residences and in the New Age sports pubs, stadiums and arenas have become more than mere sports venues; they are now veritable destinations for sports and entertainment, with the emphasis on *entertainment*. Going to the game implies a lot more than watching the game. From team owners and stadium developers to the sports leagues and sponsors, all parties involved are committed to enforcing a multisensory overload experience. Bigger is better, and *more* is definitely better. Digital monitors are constantly vying for our attention and our dollar. Craft cocktails and brews are available to satisfy our sophisticated taste buds. Hot dogs and crackerjack? No siree, nowadays only the finest farm-to-table ingredients make up the menu at the concession stands. The line between sports as a unique genre with a specific focus on athletic prowess and sports as fairground entertainment is blurred like never before. Stadiums and arenas are becoming the contemporary equivalent of nineteenth-century fairs and carnivals. We go to stadiums for the modern version of the human cannonball but also we are there to be seen and delight our senses with the sounds, sights, and tastes on display. We go to socialize, observe, and take part in an event that brings us together and threads a common bond. The bearded lady, the circus freaks, the (*insert team name*) city dancers, and T-shirt cannons are all there to entertain us, to make us lose ourselves in the mayhem. Game tickets are used as corporate perks, as a method to seal the deal and conduct business.

The stadia of yesteryear were primarily known as the locations and the hosts of athletic events, games, and tournaments, places were you had no business going to unless you were a die-hard fan or were looking to be part of a larger-than-life sports phenomenon. The focus of the discourse in the arenas has shifted from conversations about the actual game, the players, and teams playing in front of our eyes to small chatter about the myriad distractions around: the food, the drinks, the mascots, the kids' game at intermission, the DJs. And repeat. Nowadays, you are more likely to deal with topics related to the location of the Shake Shack closest to the 200-level seats than to discuss the lineup selection, rotation, matchups, or standings.

There is something for everyone in the modern stadium. Long gone are the days when sports were addressed to a specific segment of society looking for an escape. All family members are welcomed. Come on down, it is warm, cozy, and delicious inside. There is even a game on if you are so inclined.

There may just be some collateral damage from this boom in the sports as entertainment trend. The traditional fan whose eyes are glued to the field of play is essentially forced into early retirement as a participant in the discourse. This fan archetype with strong ties to the essence of the game is being priced out, unable to see and feel the game live, deprived of the live spectator experience and reduced to an ever-frustrated human heap on a couch, eyes glued to a screen, mumbling axioms about the lost beauty of The Game *"and all these damn kids on their MySpace, YourSpace, Facebooks and Instagrams."*

The Golden Era of Sports

A<small>FTER A BRIEF</small> walkabout through the hazy history of sports coverage and consumption, we are finally here, in the Year of the Lord 2016, at the confluence of a social and digital medial revolution. The cacophony of voices, links, tweets, snaps, blogs, video highlights, and live game feeds makes up the ecosystem of sports coverage and consumption.

The basic premise of these pages is the notion that we live in the Golden Age of Sports. Presumably, the same could have been said of all previous eras. By definition each technological innovation supplants the prior, inferior state of affairs. As we saw in the previous pages, television, radio, and newspapers brought sports to the masses and paved the way for the current culture of sports consumption as a main leisure activity and discussion topic.

The modern experience of consuming sports has been amplified like never before by an enormous supply of live broadcasting content, while also complemented by an infinite amount of commentary: pregame, in-game, and postgame analysis; blogging; and constant feedback through social media. This multitude of sources allows us to partake in a social bonding phenomenon, and enabling us to create our own personalized experiences simultaneously. We are at a glorious confluence of digital and social media, being afforded opportunities to watch, observe, digest and comment in real time, as well as on our own time and place. Being a sports fan in 2016 presumes being a part of, and thriving in, a social and digital ecosystem. Once you, the modern fan, enter and inhabit this ecosystem, the odds of survival in the old-school environment, deprived of the all forms of modern media, are similar to a snowman's prospects of walking across the Sahara Desert.

Can the sports consumption experience get any better? The answer is largely a subjective one. My argument is that unless you believe in having live sports content and commentary zapped directly to the part of the cerebellum responsible for the enjoyment of sports content, absent any processing and dissemination, this *is* as good as it gets. We are in that happy medium where any kind of content is readily accessible in stunning detail, complimented by niche coverage providing you with exactly the type of commentary and analysis perfectly suited for your specific taste and fandom inclinations. Given the embarrassment of sports broadcasting riches, we may already be at the tipping point. Before we get inundated with content, we have to keep in mind that part of what makes sports both exceptional and exciting as a form of entertainment is the scarcity, the unique nature of each inimitable play, highlight or event. There is only so much content we as living, breathing humans can consume before reaching diminishing returns in terms of enjoyment per minute spent in front of a TV, tablet or live at the stadium. The constant bombardment by live game content and pre- and postgame analysis is becoming off putting, with questionable effects on our attention span as well as our overall desire and demand to consume sporting content. Ratings seem to support this notion. According to a Sports *News Media* study[7], the time each self-described American sports fan spent consuming sports decreased from 8.1 and 8.3 hours per week in 2012 and 2013 respectively, to 7.7 hours per week in 2014. It appears we have reached a sweet spot, and any subsequent increases in consumption would be minimal.

In the US market, there are only so many untapped newbies and novices who represent the fertile ground for ratings expansion.

---

7 *Global Sports Media Consumption Report – 2014*, Sports News Media, Kantar Media Sports, SportsBusiness Group, May 2014

What can be better than having access to any sporting event, anytime and anywhere? The only thing that might enhance your experience as a fan is the ability to summon live commentary, analysis, and endless jokes with your fingertips. Well, guess what? We got that too. Thus closes the feedback loop and begins your modern day peak-level spectator adventure. We have it all.

What We Talk about When We Talk about Sports

A T THIS POINT in our journey through the sports consumption maze, it might be wise to take a small break and talk about the product being consumed: *The What*. After all, no matter how great the means of consumption may be, if the product being consumed lacks appeal and quality then the entire experience is ruined.

What are we looking at? What are all the voices and talking heads discussing? What is this object of affection that we spend so much time and energy on?

From a pop culture angle, modern sports are a function of the modern athlete as superstar and public figure. Modern athletes are now receiving the kind of notoriety previously reserved for movie stars, royalty, and heads of state.

The modern athletes are bigger, faster, craftier, and arguably wiser than ever before. They are groomed and conditioned to become finely tuned machines, true masters of their craft. Any comparison between players or teams across historical eras is a futile exercise. Athletes are better trained, better fed, more informed, and more dedicated to their trade. In other words, if you believe in progress, if you believe that technology, transportation, and telecommunications are nowadays superior to the way people travelled, communicated, and worked a generation ago, you are likely to buy into the notion that the spectacle on display in today's arenas and stadia is superior to what was put on display at the old, smoky "gardens" and arenas. If you are inclined to believe otherwise, you probably believe the 1965

Celts would beat the 2016 Warriors or Cavs. Good luck with that argument, ol' man.

Allowing for a few individual exceptions, the general rule of thumb is that modern professional teams and team sports generally serve a superior product. We will never know how Michael Jordan would have fared in today's NBA. Conversely, an argument can be made that Dan Marino's skills would be better suited for today's pass-happy NFL.

Take a look at grainy footage of any game from the pre-HD era. The movements were slower and more deliberate, players were allowed more time on the ball and more time to set up and go through their sets. There were no helmets, less padding, smaller men, less athletic-looking men and women. Perhaps it was a more purist, quintessentially athletic process: less emphasis on equipment and becoming a (insert sport)-playing machine, more human, more prone to errors, and easier to relate to.

Let's not digress. The point here is that the product on display is greater than ever. "Golden Era" applies to the product on display as well as the method of consumption. Some may wax nostalgic about the days of old, but in reality almost all athletic feats from the past have been surpassed. I am proposing that much like our Internet-era lifestyle, the product being consumed is faster, more exciting, and more prone to provide instant gratification than ever before.

OK, So How Do We Watch Sports?

On TVs, tablets, laptops and phones. At bars, on couches and lazy-boys, in plush box seats, dark man- caves, on trains and buses. Alone, with friends, relatives, frenemies, alongside various human beings with whom we'd have nothing else in the world to discuss if it weren't for the common object of our interest and affection.

Media outlets and technological advances allow us access to sporting events from anywhere in the world, on any of our personal portable devices and at any ungodly hour of the day. Watching a game on DVR, on your own personal viewing terms and timeline, with one eye on the sporting event and the other on the second screen,[8] with its corresponding game-related Twitter feed, or Facebook team page is both the required process for any self-respecting modern fan and also some unimaginable, sci-fi-like experience for fans belonging to the prior generation.

DVR technology accomplished in just a few short years what two decades of programmed VCR attempts could not do: allow you to relish the spectacle at a time and place of your choosing (Cue Jon Bon Jovi's jingle *The Power to Turn Back Time* from that god-awful DirecTV ad).

The lines between the live spectator experience and the broadcast experience are getting blurrier. As Smart Seats proliferate across the new generation of stadiums, fans are spending an increased amount having a game-watching experience closer to the one at-home.

The supply of sports content is inexhaustible and ubiquitous. With the advent of over-the-web broadcasting, there are limitless possibilities to partake in any sporting event in the world anytime from anywhere, as well as to read, debate, and analyze these sporting events with anyone, anywhere and ad nauseam. Name your poison, and chances are that someone, somewhere, somehow will bring it to you live. In turn, all the sports content made available spawns a never-ending supply of commentary, angles, and takes (some hot, some not so hot), all meant to capture your eyeballs and augment your fan experience by adding more layers of data and information. The collective thirst for sports can finally be quenched.

Ultimately, there are two culprits largely responsible for bringing us into the age. The disruptors and perpetrators are the two newly sprouted branches of the media tree: the digital and the social. Both

---

8 "Second Screen" is in fact the industry name for mobile device or tablet activity occurring during a television event.

of these parts are recent advances, and both are the offspring of the relatively recent Internet revolution.

We've come a long way since the rabbit ears, black and white, blackout days of the '80s.

To the sports fan raised a generation prior to the explosion in social media and the advancements in digital recording, this level of access and viewing flexibility would have seemed inconceivable. Taping the game with the click of a button and having the ability to skip through time-outs and commercial breaks? No need for stacks of videotapes or other storage devices to build a nostalgic shrine to sports heroes of glory past? The stereotypical sports fanatic of the '80s and '90s would have dismissed this as pure sci-fi baloney. The intersection of sports and technology was a very small and lonely space. Outside of spreadsheets and some cryptic predictive analytics software, the demand for technology within the sports universe was limited to the television set and the ability to control a remote control. Those were indeed simpler times.

Nowadays, it has become almost impossible to stay away from social media and include yourself as part of the discourse around sports. Even as late as the turn of the millennium, just listening to sports radio, perhaps reading the sports section, and following along semi-passively was sufficient to qualify you for what passed as sports talk. You did not have to dedicate too much effort to consider yourself suitable for sports conversation. That all began to change as soon as sports coverage became more nuanced and decentralized. Many voices began bringing forth interesting angles and takes to the discussion. Many other voices amplified the level of hate and vitriol. A lot of noise has been created, and having the ability to sift through the noise to get through to the meaningful data and the insightful takes has become a necessary skill in order to count yourself as a well-informed fan with pertinent points of view and not just another mouth-breathing jock. Social media and digital media provide access to customized data, highlights, and information, but ultimately and more importantly, these technologies introduced a level of discourse much more elevated than that of the more simplistic days of the late '90s.

Among the more notable current trends in sports content intake is consumption through voyeurism. An entire generation of up and coming sports fans have made watching *other people* watch sports an actual pastime. This is a "thing"[9]. No, it's not an actual game that we (or rather *they,* if you choose to disassociate yourself from this trend) are watching - it's the fans that are *watching* a game. Curious as it may seem, I admit that watching others' reactions to a dramatic play makes for good content. It is a pretty entertaining way to spend about…two minutes or so. Then what? If the raw emotion generated by sports is the main thing you are concerned about, is this entry-level form of voyeurism you are partaking in related to sports at all? Can you call yourself a sports fan if your sports-related intake is not in the form of actual game-footage? If dramatic reactions is what you're after why not just Netflix and chill?

Evidently, being a sports fan in 2016 means navigating through intricate streets and back alleys and peeking through the blinders. It almost makes one long for the simple and straightforward proposition of watching the one game in town, live, uninterrupted and completely focused on the performance on the field or on the screen.

Speaking of which….

What Becomes of Old-School Luddites?

Up until a decade ago, the most loyal, devoted, and knowledgeable fans I came across were the old-school types who had been witnesses to different eras and different trends in sports. With age comes wisdom, so I always made a point of discussing sports with representatives of

---

9 The main culprit is Copa90, which is a YouTube channel with over 1million followers. Copa90 dubs itself "the home of football fan culture." Content includes embedding its presenters with "Ultras" fan groups, telling the fan stories of big derby days, and showing wild fans celebrations.

the older and wiser generation, the golden boys (and girls) of sports. Unfortunately, these types of conversations across generations are a little less meaningful today, as the wise old sages have been slower to adapt and incorporate social and digital media into their sports consumption routine. At what cost, though?

Depriving yourself of access through the available digital and social media sources is the sort of quirk that you can no longer afford to have in this day and age, when real news and in-game highlights break out on Twitter faster than anywhere else. If you choose to be a social media Luddite, you are almost no longer "credentialed" to count yourself as part of the conversation. It is not that the veteran fans are less knowledgeable now than they were only a decade ago, it is more a function of the rest of the world catching up. There is an encyclopedia of sports information available at your fingertips. Maybe you and I were not there when Bucky Dent hit his three-run homer in 1978, but we sure heard the reference enough times, and if we are interested in baseball at all, we have seen enough highlights, documentaries, and commentaries to paint a pretty good image and evoke emotions the likes of which would not have been possible except through word of mouth from middle-aged guys with names like Sal or Lou, who all remember where they were when that happened. But now there is hardly any need at all to talk to the old heads and get their thoughts and feelings on an event, when we can summon a 30-minute documentary on virtually any topic, within seconds.

The well-connected fan knows to look for clues in order to assess credibility on the other side of the sports discourse. Any talk about "passing fads" when it comes to media and technology had better be limited if you have any hope of being taken seriously as a knowledge-able sports fan. Tread carefully; one too many jokes about "no damn snapping" or tweeting and you can be sure that any old school fan cred you might have had will be relegated to the dustbin of history.

On the other hand, if you do find yourself continuing to seek the same basic, untainted emotion, free of any social media influence and blog-head hot takes, the experience that only live sports in their pure and primal format can offer—I salute you; you are an OG, a veteran. You are an almost extinct breed, the wooly mammoth of sports fans. You need protection and understanding. We appreciate what you bring.

The Rise of the New Sports Order

As for the rest of us, on the output side, social media has given us a voice or, at the very least, the impression that we have a voice. It is a blunt instrument that can be used to achieve a certain level of notoriety. Perhaps more importantly, on the intake side, we have access to peruse, or binge on an infinite supply of content spanning the gamut from homeristic[10] fan sites to highbrow sports literature.

Although the collective social media public at large, the consumers and users of information, have been called nerds, losers, or worse (looking at you, Charles Barkley), we have to remember that this comes with the territory, and ultimately it is a relatively small price to pay for this level of content, access, and ability to interact with pundits and athletes alike. Yes, there are many bad apples in the form of angry mouth-breathing jerks who sometimes ruin it for the rest of us by abusing this freedom and the right to troll, but don't let that prevent you from joining ranks with civilization and becoming a part of the social media ecosystem.

Digital media has provided channels to infinite access to the teams we support, rendering location irrelevant. We have *ALL* the access. Technological advances have exacerbated the sports discourse, exposed and enabled an assortment of fan types who collectively participate in one of modern America's favorite pursuits—the sports discourse. For those sports fans that cut their teeth in the era of television

---

10 As in "homer" – the type of fan who is highly biased and will argue on behalf of his favorite team in the face of clear evidence to the contrary. No relation to Homer, the Greek author of *The Iliad*.

highlights, nightly news sports updates and next day newspaper coverage, it is important to realize that that particular fan experience has
gone the way of the dinosaurs. There really is no "fan cred" associated
with being an "old-school" fan, the type that gets their sports fix by
waiting for the late SportsCenter edition and getting his/her sports
coverage from the sports section of the local newspaper. Being old
school in terms of fandom does not carry the allure that being an "old
school" artist whose craft is timeless. We all need to adapt and realize
that the era of centralized sports coverage is over, that the experience
of tuning in to Keith Olbermann and Dan Patrick for the news of the
day and hear the comforting puns that became part of pop culture
in the mid 90s cannot be replicated today. Lacking the excitement
and anticipation of breaking news and highlights, any sports highlight
show is doomed to get annihilated by the Twittersphere.

Live games aside, sports networks are faced with the prospect of
hemorrhaging audience numbers[11] unless they are able to replace
the traditional highlight show with compelling content that will
make you, the fan, sacrifice your social media attention in favor
of television sports programming. Enter fabricated controversies,
ridiculous game show-type programming with epilepsy-inducing
flashing lights, beeps and horns (looking at you, *Around the Horn*),
talking heads with zany opinions meant to stir up your emotions.
Traditionally, sports coverage was a form of entertainment and
escapism. With the clutter of sports content available, it is easy to
feel suffocated and perhaps overwhelmed. In times of exasperation
with the current sports content landscape, it serves to remember
why you are drawn to sports in the first place. If you feel your blood
pressure going up and your teeth clenching at the sight of Skip
Bayless, fret not, dear friend, this is a normal reaction. It is time
to switch the dial before you fall in to the trap laid out before you.

---

11 Total Television screen time has decreased 3% Year over Year, while time spent on
social media has increased 25% as of 2013, according to a Nielsen Study.

Walk away. Sports commentary programming is not meant to get your blood boiling. You are better than this.

Each one of us embraces the spectator experience differently, in a way as unique as our individual outlook on life or personal belief system. Our expectations and demands from the sporting spectacle are as unique and wide ranging as we are as individuals. Maybe you watch sports to escape reality; maybe you want to understand the read option, the Cover 2 defense, or the Princeton offense. You might just crave that type of football and basketball porn in your life. Perhaps you have a fifty-spot on St. Bonaventure tonight or need a few points from a random backup running back to beat your frenemy in fantasy football.

How we ended up being the sports fans that we are today hinges on two main factors: our psychological makeup and our early individual experiences that shaped us as fans. Nature versus nurture, baby. While some of us are predisposed to moping and misery, others grew up as fans of the Chicago Bulls and Dallas Cowboys in the '90s. If you were about that Michael Jordan life, never-ending glory was the norm. Titles and glory were all you knew. You came into adult fandom expecting rings and trophies. If, on the other hand, you happened to be a part of that cursed fan segment known as "the JIM" (Jets, Islanders, Mets) or happened to be from either one of the majestic cities of Cleveland, Buffalo, Minneapolis you probably learned the hard way that there wouldn't be a ticker-tape parade this year. Or the next one, either. This is to say that the way each one of us interprets sport and participates in the discourse was largely shaped by our formative experiences as fans.

In the following section, I invite you to go through some fan archetypes.

Unique personality types aside, there are some general archetypes that I have always found amusing. With the advent of both digital and social media, these archetypes have been exacerbated. Clearly, the categories below are not mutually exclusive; there is a significant overlap among these types. I am not advocating that a person should be pigeonholed as one, singular type of fan at all times, but for argument's sake, we are keeping the archetypes separated and unique. The portraits painted below are caricatures. The unique traits of each archetype have been intentionally exaggerated to highlight the quirkiness and uniqueness of each piece of the sports fandom puzzle. Each of us brings along a personal viewpoint to help shape the landscape and the market for sports consumption. As a fan with strong feelings, you may find some characteristics of a certain archetype (not the one you might belong to) loathsome. Take a deep breath, and remember that between these covers, we are in a judgment-free zone.

For the most part these fan types are meant to make light of the new and strong crops of fans, sprouted from the fertile ground of the post-internet world. My hope is that each of the subsequent fan depictions instills a heightened sense of self-awareness allowing you to become a more polished sports fan. Arguably, self-awareness and ability to capture nuance are instruments required to generate a more complete, elevated experience of fandom and sports consumption.

How Social and Digital Media
Define the Modern Fan Archetypes

The Sports Savant

"That's the wonderful thing with nerds: They're enthusiasts. Not having a life means you get to love things with a passion, and nobody bothers you about it"

(JOHN BURNSIDE, SCOTTISH WRITER)

THESE GUYS ARE not in it for the fun. Entertainment and escape are not the things that come to mind when the game is being played. By definition, the savant is a man of numbers, formulas, science, and big brains. Sports may not necessarily be in his blood; but they sure have turned out to be an optimal avenue to showcase the savant's intellect. The brain is the muscle that this fan archetype feels compelled to put on display in the aftermath of any purely emotional, joyous play. The savant's implicit intention is to shift the emotion-filled sporting discourse to a rational, joyless dialogue. In the event of a breathtaking play, the dialogue may go something like this:

"Oh, man, you see that catch? Holy shit!"
"Well, the corner blew the coverage, and he didn't get any help over the top from the safety, so yeah, not surprised."
"Umm, bruh, the catch!"

He's not a fan of the highlight reel and is extremely difficult to impress with visual stimuli. He approaches every event with a slightly smug, superior air. He is the hipster of sports. This man has seen some things, and he is sure to let you know about it. Very little, if anything, will surprise him. He reads highbrow websites (less ESPN, Barstool sports and local sports media, more Grantland(RIP), The Ringer, Football Outsiders, The Blizzard Mag) and listens to podcasts that mention things like *standard deviation* and *regression from the mean*.

He is not in it for the joy or the bonding element of sports. He is rarely a fan of the big-ticket teams and gravitates to underdogs. Cool and composed, he is interested in *The Process,* the behind-the-scenes aspects of sports and team management: the recruiting, the contract negotiations, the salary cap implications, and modern trends in the game. Needless to say, he's a stat head and will try to shift any sports discourse away from the emotional aspects of sports and toward the abstract. He would prefer to boil down any discussion about sports to a mathematical equation or algorithm. Sloan Conference talk will be had; any sanguine excitement in the room will be reduced to the lowest analytical common denominator.

This type of fan has had the most to benefit from in the explosion of sports analytics and the coverage of various statistical trends in sports media, of the social or traditional kind. This begs the question as to the whereabouts or existence of the sports savant in the pre-Internet era. Much like his non-sports-fan equivalent, the hipster, this specimen has multiplied exponentially and makes up a significant portion of the spectator scene.

His general knowledge and genuine interest are a net positive influence on the fandom landscape. Sports have benefited from his presence; His genuine curiosity in the sporting equivalent of "sausage making" has uncovered many previously hidden aspects of game strategy, tactics and even franchise management.

<u>Spectating habits:</u>

For the most part just a casual observer, the sports savant would rather devote more time to the research and study of the game than to actual viewing of game action. As the relationship with sports is a complicated one, he is not likely to watch a random regular season game, the exception being if one of the teams *du jour* is showcased, in which case he will spend the time not so much watching the game as looking for the unique angle underlining his deep understanding of the game. Exciting games and great teams will come and go; the savant's intellectual expertise is everlasting.

We are not likely to encounter this specimen attending live games in the modern, sensory-overload arenas. Live, in-stadium viewing appeals to the emotional and visceral, taking us away from the analytical and the abstract, also known as the sports savant's comfort zones. Typically, the savant is not seeking out that emotional bonding experience as a part of his game-watching ritual. The notches on his fandom belt have been pierced by sharp little nuggets of wisdom and anecdotes sourced from #sportsanalytics Twitter, not from any ticket stubs or selfies taken at the game. It is difficult to say what exactly it is about the sport that he enjoys. If cockroach racing or dueling robots had the same mass appeal and sabermetrics behind them, we would find the savant expounding the same empirical theories with regard to the creepy-crawly's sprint style or the salary cap implications related to signing an outdated robot with outdated armor material and fighting style.

He prefers watching the games in the comfort of his home, with multiple viewing angles, personalized snack options, and most importantly, full access to online research and social media platforms.

Social Media Impact:

We can safely attribute the sports savants population boom to social media. The correlation is perfect, the causality spot on. The significance of the newly found ability to transmit information, to quip and wax poetic about random statistics gathered through the Twittersphere cannot be understated. His social media activity is mostly confined to the well-curated list of like-minded pundits.

Our sports savant is able to source the esoteric nuggets and random sports facts that are only to be brought to light during cocktail parties. There is an argument to be made that our little sporty hipster savant owes his existence to the explosion of social media and smartphones.

As his regard for sports is a more cerebral kind of affection, the savant needed the unlimited data dumps available online to be able to construct theories, angles, and twists. He may not be in it for the love of the game, but through the constant theorizing, the scientific approach, devoid and untainted by any visceral emotions, he has unveiled a more elevated level of discourse. As irritating as it may be to give the nerds their due, this kind of contribution really does make sports more interesting.

The Romantic Loyalist

"...So please, be tolerant of those who describe a sporting moment as their best ever. We do not lack imagination, nor have we had sad and barren lives; it is just that real life is paler, duller, and contains less potential for unexpected delirium."

(NICK HORNBY, FEVER PITCH)

LOVE OF TEAM logo, crest, and colors runs deep here. Heavy on emotional attachment, this quintessential fan type represents what had been known as *the stereotype.*

Up until a decade ago, when sports media and coverage became more nuanced and sophisticated, the loyalist was your couch potato slob, tuning in to every game, emotionally invested all the way. The good guys belonged to him and his; the bad guys were the others. It was and still is a simple world. Life is complicated enough as it is. Why bother with nuance; why peel the onion layers when all you want is a simple pleasure? Just win, baby. And hey, if you don't, it's OK. Tomorrow is another day, and there's always next season.

This fan may have inherited the affiliation through family ties, but once hooked, he was *All In,* with the kind of obsession and love reserved for the most sacred things in life. This type would be more likely to cheat on a spouse than be dishonest about his rooting interest or (God forbid) switch over to another outfit. Always positive, he remains optimistic in the face of adversity (*read: losing*). Criticizing the object of his affection is akin to treason. The loyalist is a man of strong character, oftentimes seeing himself as an ambassador or even an extension of the team he bleeds for. Very transparent, he is not here to play your mind games or contemplate the place of sports fandom in your universe. He just wants a W, dammit.

Unfortunately, due to his transparent nature, he usually gets a bad rap. This is the archetype easiest to mock and caricaturize; this is the college jock with huge pecs and pea-size brain, the sloppy, middle-aged loser with the team logo attire (sweatpants a must) pounding a six-pack and yelling at the screen in a dark room or man cave of sorts.

Having devoted so much time, effort, energy, and money, his daily emotional state is driven by the fortunes and performances of the team. The team takes a loss, and he already knows he's about to toss and turn all night pondering *"what if?"* and *"shoulda, woulda, coulda."* The team wins the game, and it is sweet dreams all the way, baby! He knows he's going to wake up smiling. Emotionally, the romantic idealist becomes one with the team. Its wins are his wins; its losses ruin days and nights. It's pretty simple, really. All these new fads don't concern him. All those blogs, online prospectuses, and Twitter tatter is for the boys who never played the game. *Analytics are for limp-wristed sissy boys who could never hit a fastball and never strapped the pads on. You can either hit a ball or not, and ain't no mathematical formulas going to change that.

Suffice to say that the boom in game data and inside analysis during and after the game does not appeal to the romantic loyalist. He has no use for them. The game is played on the field, not on a spreadsheet.

Spectating habits:

All of them. He loves all the games. If it's on, he will be there, remote in hand, ready to live and die by the side of his idols. He sacrifices personal time and commitments in order to *be there* for the team. Whether he is in his seat at the stadium or watching live at home, this man is the one upon whom social media has the least impact. Uninterested in the totality of data and information available through multiple sources, his attention is razor-sharp, focused on the action unfolding live in front of his eyes. Consuming data and nuggets of information sourced through social media does nothing but distract him. He has very limited appreciation for a better-rounded, more complex game-watching experience. Peeling the onion layers to understand the driving forces *and reasons behind a game's final outcome is not something he is interested in. He's big on the eye test and has no use for analytics and the accompanying sports geeks.

The DVR and any modern viewing options and experiences have not changed his viewing habits—live, as it happens, no distractions. The RedZone channel may be something he tinkers with eventually, but definitely not while his favorite team is playing live on network TV.

He is the type who would (gladly) miss a dinner, a birthday party, a wedding, to be in front of the TV wearing his lucky Gildan sweat-pants, rooting on his boys.

High definition, big screen broadcasts? *I want me some of that!* - The technological advances that he has any use for are the extra pixels and the big screen, the centerpiece of any man cave sanctuary. He'll dabble in new tech as long as it amplifies the existing experience, without introducing any new elements or nuance to his ritual.

Given the current emphasis on parity in American sports, this fan type has been through some exhilarating ups but especially some painful downs, which leads to one of his dirty secrets, the thousand-pound gorilla in the room. He needs to numb the pain and amplify any exhilaration stemming from a W. The romantic idealist fan would gladly trade any Twitter handle for a six-pack. The bottle is always close, an integral part of the full game day experience. This is the fan archetype most likely to partake in a full-on, obsessive-compulsive game day ritual. Lucky undies, socks, and the T-shirt worn during the 1987 conference title game must be worn. Pregame snacks and their sequencing and timing must always be consistent. The in-game *feng shui* needs to be followed and strictly respected. There will be no disruption in body positioning, no movement during a good spell of play or a scoring drive. You have to hold it in. Momentum must be preserved at all costs, even if it could result in soiling your undies.

Sci-Fi Utilitarian

"A dollar won is twice as sweet as a dollar earned"

(Paul Newman, "Color of Money")

THIS CATEGORY IS the polar opposite of the romantic loyalist. This person has zero feelings for you and your team. She (let's make this as a fan of the fairer gender, for conversation's sake) is a by-product of the explosion of online fantasy sports and Internet gambling. She couldn't care less about any highlight reel unless it suits his purposes and can generate some form of revenue. Our girl is all about those benjamins.

We could be a witnessing a transcendent play, a once-in-a-generation event, but unless the athlete or team performing it is fully aligned with her fantasy team or playing for the team that she's got a stake on, she has no use it for it. She would rather gain a few bucks than feel any communal joy. This begs the question of whether this specimen is ruining sports as we've traditionally grown to appreciate and follow them. Once we accept that sporting events exist purely for his practical reasons, we are essentially using sports in the same way you use your eTrade account.

Traditionally, this spectator segment has been on the fringe, relegated to the backs of bar rooms and basements where the sports gambling degenerates of the day gathered around, pen and paper in hand, to pick winners of the games and draft faceless players on their make-believe teams. The sci-fi utilitarian is completely desensitized to the fact that there are real life human beings with families, feelings, and their own livelihoods at stake. They have come to consider athletes as replaceable widgets partaking in little parlor games. This is the purely capitalist version of sports fans, all about the bottom line, profits, and losses, with no actual regard to human emotion, feelings, or social activism.

The relatively recent boom in the ranks of fantasy players and gamblers can be traced back to the boardrooms and offices of professional sports leagues, where a conscious effort was made to make fans feel *invested* in the game. The NFL in particular has made efforts to market player data in order for the public at large to package and compile it for fantasy purposes; the league has also been changing the game rules to benefit offensive outputs so that stats become inflated. There is also a cognitive effect in play here—once the utilitarian-to-be begins to feel that she owns the players, she begins being more devoted and attached, following and tuning in to games even more, bearing witness live to the performances of *her* players.

According to the Fantasy Sports Trade Association—a marketing and advocacy organization focused on fantasy sports—approximately forty-two million people played fantasy sports in 2014, up from thirty-two million players in 2010. About 70 percent of fantasy sports players listed football as their favorite fantasy game, so at least thirty million people played fantasy football in 2014—about 13 percent of the total adult population of the United States. The average fantasy sports player spends nine hours per week on the game. As far as dollars and sense are concerned, according to Advertising Age magazine, fantasy football generated $1.1 billion in revenue in 2013.

This is serious business. Let us also keep in mind that the numbers above predate the boom in daily fantasy sports.

Spectating habits:

Fully connected to all media types and streams, the fantasy player needs complete access to stats and information at all times. Her live daily fantasy feed's results need to be updated obsessively. Not a play goes by without the refresh semicircle being tapped.

The advent of smartphone apps promoting and allowing access to thousands of fantasy contests every hour of the day is the crack pipe she needs. There is never any supply shortage for this degenerate addict, with the constant barrage of ads on all the relevant media outlets. All she needs is a couple of bucks and a few taps on the screen, and she's got the shot right in the vein.

She shares some of the viewing habits of the sports savant, in the sense that both of these categories of sports followers (as opposed to sports *fans*) bring an analytical approach, seeking out the value plays and the hidden angles, which in this case could be construed as winning plays. It is likely that the utilitarian type is even more removed from the emotional experience of the athletic spectacle unfolding on the screen or any individual performers. This "What can you do for me?" attitude borders on the psychotic. Players are reduced to metrics and corresponding salaries, indexed values over average contribution and matchup performances versus specific opponents. We could be witnessing the greatest, most unique highlight reel in history, the utilitarian might not even bat an eyelash before hitting that little refresh button checking if that play had any impact of consequence on her $3 DraftKings daily entry.

In all fairness, we owe a lot to this segment. Her way of dissecting the game to make a buck has created a demand for in-depth coverage and has made the public at large more familiar with players who have been more on the fringe of the game than in the spotlight.

Even if you completely remove yourself from this category of fans, it is likely that you have seen one too many DraftKings ads to resist temptation or have been a part of a traditional fantasy league. Fantasy games have one (or three or five) winners but many, many more losers. Chances are that this hobby took some sort of a hit on your wallet.

On the other hand and on a less-obvious sports fandom level, chances are that without a vested interested in some obscure midseason game, you and I would have missed out on moments of real live sporting excitement and highlights of the game.

The Contrarian Cynic

*"The four most beautiful words in our common language: I
told you so"*

(GORE VIDAL)

THIS SPECIMEN MIGHT just be the most fascinating one of all. Twisted
and complicated, his affinity and sometimes love of the game cannot be questioned. The same cannot be said for his love of any particular team.

He loves to separate herself from the pack of *other* sports fans by
constantly going against the grain. Sports are only interesting to him
if there is an angle against common wisdom to be taken.

By nature, there is very little fundamentally right or wrong in
sports; for the most part, referees implement the rules of the game,
and the scoreboard is the one thing that metes out true justice. In the
time between games, we sports fans are generally comfortable navigating in a vast gray area, speculating about what the ideal course
of action would be in order for a given team to be successful. We
theorize, opine, and ideate about the right direction of the franchise.
This is part of what makes sports fun. We enjoy moonlighting as GMs,
team owners, and coaches and have grand delusions about "righting
the ship" or taking teams to new heights of glory. Whatever opinion
we happen to hold, the contrarian will debate us on it. He will question our hypothesis and bring up real-life examples in which similar
theories failed miserably. His nihilism is well versed; he is not here to
provide solutions or constructive criticism, rather seeking to destroy
and shit on your ticker-tape-parade dreams. The seeds of doubt are
sown early and often, cultivated carefully along the way, only to be
reaped when whatever theory or grand plan for success we concocted
through conversations inevitably fails, as is often the case. The math
is clear, and it always works in the cynic's favor-most teams will not
win the big one this year, next year, or in a generation, will not even
make the playoffs, so there are vast opportunities to gloat over the

misery of others. The contrarian cynic is playing with house money, baby.

Being a fan implies hitching your wagon to the fortunes of a team and associating with its respective strategy for success. It is self-defeating, futile, and exhausting to oppose the tactical direction of the team you support. You are a fan, you want to *believe*.

Well, that's too bad. The contrarian cynic cannot wait to drop that *I told you so* on you. Not having any emotional investment in any team, hi true rooting interest is against the popular opinion. All his joy is derived from seeing bandwagons disintegrate and seasons implode[12].

Assuming you don't find yourself in this category, it's very likely you have been given numerous fair warnings that your team's star player is injury prone, that the style of offense employed is outdated, that the owner is a gigantic asshole that doesn't care about you or the success of the franchise. If you had just heeded the warnings (read: negativity) of the contrarian, you could have saved yourself the trouble and the heartache.

Spectating habits:

The cynic needs a venue to make her cynicism public, and social media has come along to provide just this type of stage. Watching alone, without an audience, in the privacy of his home serves little purpose unless there is a strong army of social media followers behind. Her strong, contrarian opinions must be heard, documented, and validated. He can't really proclaim "*I told you so*" to himself. It defeats the purpose, and it may lead to schizophrenia.

His social media presence must be prolific and on point. The Twittersphere makes up a huge well of like-minded individuals and opinion, and our contrarian hero is thirsty. He will indulge drinking from that #itoldyouso well. His opinions are often times shaped

---

12 I consciously avoided using "hater" to describe the contrarian. Although they share a lot of characteristics, the contrarian is a subtler version of the "hater".

by 140-character blurbs shared by bloggers with the same cynical inclinations.

A big conspiracy theorist, the contrarian cynic scours the internets for evidence that a call was missed, a game was rigged, and is a big proponent of the argument that there are always greater powers at play. He loves sending gifs and vines to his gang of non-believers to prove a point that goes against the grain. By providing infinite resources of data and viewpoints to support his arguments, social media has enabled this individual and has given him the tools to blossom.

Social Butterfly

"Football, now, it becomes about the people you watch the games with."

(IRVINE WELSH, FEBRUARY 2, 2016)

EVER SINCE THE dawn of spectator sports and events, communities have been built among the flock of local fans and lifelong friendships and families have been borne out of shared rooting interests. It's a beautiful thing, really.

In the modern era, as the line between sports bars and night clubs gets blurrier, going out to watch a game is becoming a revelry, a night out. With clubby names and fancy drink and food menus, these nightlife destinations are capitalizing on the increased reach of sports and our basic need to feel a sense of belonging, especially given the transient, faceless nature of big city life.

Within large urban areas, the current sports Public House trends emphasize comfort and glitz over grit and authenticity,[13] giving rise to a sports fan category that prizes the social benefits of game -viewing above all other aspects of fandom. These are the modern men and women for whom sports make up the *lingua franca*, the common ground and language that brings them together. Sporting events matter to this group as they allow its members to step up their social game, meet people, and forge relationships. Two major developments can be blamed for the proliferation of sports bars, the modern, posh versions of houses of worship for the modern fan:

First, we have the high-definition TV era as a major catalyst bringing about the sports pub revolution. It's difficult to imagine going out and congregating around a 27-inch standard television set. There would be a very limited area that would be afforded a good enough view of the action. Unless you were within a few feet of a standard definition set, it would have been impossible to have a good grasp of

---

13 I am referring here to the traditional spectating experience, where *The Game* mattered most, as opposed to the atmosphere or the quality of bar snacks or bar clientele.

the action on the field or the court. Even the words *standard definition* sound ancient, reminders of closed chapters, dusty barrooms, peanut shells on the floor, and fandom eras long gone.

The second factor is the quality of the offerings on tap and in the kitchen. Less of the watered-down Buds and fake potato chips and more of the fortified craft brews and Wagyu beef burgers. Sight, taste, smell—all the senses must be pleased.

Combine these two elements, and you get the boom in the sports bar scene, the explosion of Buffalo Wild Wings, Champs, Bounce, and the rest.

While viewing options have become much more accessible, going out to watch a game is not quite the simple activity it used to be. We have gained large, crystal-clear, high-definition screens bringing to life exceptional visual quality. The stadium atmosphere is now replicable in a large barroom featuring a ten-foot HD projector screen and noisy crowds pounding drinks at will. These are all net positives; I would love to have had all these viewing options back when there was only one standard definition small screen TV around that didn't offer any additional game options to what was already available in the comfort of your own home. In a public setting, the spectating game done changed, though. You now have the ability to watch any game, in any sport, in crisp HD, on a larger screen than what you have at home, while enjoying a craft brew, comfortably situated on a plush seat. Life is good, baby.

And yet…and yet we have lost something. All that comfort and fine social living has taken the focus away from the main feature. The purist in me argues that we have reached the tipping point of social spectating. The attention to the game is secondary, at best. With all the sensory overload in the modern era sports bars, we are losing sight of the sporting spectacle, the original focus point and object of our affection. Once the game has become the secondary or tertiary focal point of our social group activity, it's fair to ask whether we still need sports as an excuse to meet up. Having been a part of numerous events that had sports-watching as the main pretext for a meet up, it amazes me how little time and attention is actually devoted to the game, once the social butterflies with a penchant for athletic events have all gathered around.

Spectating habits:
This fan archetype requires not only optimal viewing conditions, but also a long list of other requirements meant to bring the viewing experience closer to what a night of clubbing was in the '80s or '90s. We (or they) want to be seen, we want to be trendy, we want to consume delicious cocktails and locally sourced pigs in blankets.

Yes, the game needs to be on, definitely in HD with an unimpeded view, but more importantly, the beer needs to be crafty and cold, the hors d'oeuvres had better be locally sourced, coming from an haute cuisine. The clientele needs to be *fine*. We now care about what we wear to the sports bar. We are here for the game, sure, but we also want to be noticed and make memories that last longer than the imprint of last night's box score in our minds. The social butterfly is here to party, to meet people, and to hook up, while the game serves as the ideal background.

Specific to this general archetype, you might argue that the approach to game viewing tends to vary by gender. Clearly diverging viewing habits split across gender lines may have been the case a generation ago, but to the trained eye, the spectating habits of men and women have become more similar, blurring gender lines. You will encounter highly devoted, fanatical lady fans that genuinely care about the game while at the same time keeping an eye out for that eye candy in the corner.

At the same time and locale, you should be able to spot the dude who has given up on Tinder and has jumped on the local squad's bandwagon, not because of the exciting fast-paced small ball or the shutdown defense, but because he is well aware that the modern day (or modern night, rather) sports bar is where the party is at. It's a nighttime destination and a *scene*. Going out to watch the ball game implies carrying along intentions that go beyond a team-rooting interest and may or may not be as pure as they seem to the old school–type fan's eye. Our social butterfly fan is here to outkick his coverage, baby!

Fortunately, the gilded confines of the modern sports bar serve as the perfect backdrop for a memorable evening of cocktails, gastro pub fare, and flirting. And oh yeah, there also happens to be a game on that seventy-inch, 4K screen there.

VI. A la Carte Sports Fan—Zipi, Alex, and the Leaders of the New School

"Live sports man…it's like a drug"

(ZIPI TORRES, INTERNATIONAL MAN OF MYSTERY AND
FANDOM, MAY 2016)

Two-THIRTY IN THE morning in Madrid. The graveyard shift is about to begin. Alarm clock rings discreetly. Zipi Torres shushes his wife back to sleep and stumbles over to the living room where some *patatas bravas* and an endless stream of *Rojadirecta* links and various satellite channels of questionable legality are waiting. The 'Canes are about to kick off in a primetime battle against their bitter rivals, FSU. The warm voice of Brent Musburger announces itself in the headphones, while the glow of the laptop screen gently caresses his face. This is home. This is the warm bosom of comfort awaiting him in the wee hours of every weekend.

Zipi Torres is a member of a growing segment of international fans who gather virtually in chat groups and through social media hashtags, a bond and support system as deep and strong as the loyalty to their favorite team. It just so happens that their loyalties lie with a franchise thousands of miles away. This dedication goes beyond the need to fill an emotional void or to be part of a victorious bandwagon. This is a long-distance relationship, at times complicated, with an object of affection that suits his needs in a much more personal way than any of the local teams would ever be able to.

Nine o'clock on a cold Sunday night in Bucharest. Parental duties fulfilled, Alex retires in front of the television. The Romanian commentators are having a field day mixing up their sports metaphors. Soccer parlance doesn't quite apply to American football commentary. Amused, yet mildly annoyed, Alex hits "mute" and settles in for a divisional playoff round matchup of his newly found guilty pleasure, the NFL.

These are just a few examples in a growing segment of long-distance fandom that is having the kind of transcontinental fandom affairs that would have been impossible less than a generation ago.

Just as digital technology and media are making long-distance relationships more likely to thrive, so does access to NBA League Pass NFL GameDay, NHL Center Ice, and MLB.TV. These are the fans' equivalents of Skype and FaceTime. Just log in to your app, seek out the object of your affection, and settle in for a close encounter of the first kind.

This type of relationship also applies to the disenfranchised fan. A quarter century ago, if your Cardinals, Colts, or Browns left town they essentially vanished from your life. Without any local TV coverage, maintaining a rooting interest in an out-of-market franchise was at best a tall order and at worst an impossible task. Any team that moved locations did so leaving behind a jilted fan base, a trail of destruction, and an empty crater of a stadium. Even if you were willing to overlook the team ownership's treacherous ways, the struggle to keep up with your former hometown heroes, the team that taught you what fandom and loyalty meant was very real. Any regional, provincial aspects of fandom have been greatly diluted. The clannish, cult-like aspect of a Green Bay Cheesehead or Alabama football fan (#rolltide) may still exist, but it is now conceivable that the same level of passion and obsession can be garnered from anywhere on the planet. Long distance relationships are now finally possible. Going away to college does not imply an emotional breakup any longer. Job changes requiring relocations offer the benefit of bringing along the object of your sporting affections. Sure, you can sniff around and sow your oats in whatever local sports scene you may be residing in, but you know that your first and true love will always be there for you, one League Pass or Sunday Ticket away. Fandom promiscuity is not encouraged, and the tools to stay true and faithful to your main squeeze are all there for you, a click of a button away.

In 1991, I was a fan of one team and one team only, a romantic loyalist with the best of them. Steaua Bucharest represented the center of my fandom existence. I couldn't imagine ever rooting for another squad. She was my one and only. Over time, through repeated exposure to other local teams and higher quality coverage, I learned to love again. Fan polygamy became a thing. Digital media brought us back together a decade later. We were both involved in steady relationships by then. We each had built up some baggage and became jaded participants in the fan - franchise dating game. I knew where I stood, and was content having an open relationship, consumed online through live stream links and social media banter. We were a huge part of each other's past and now, through the unlimited powers of digital and social media, our present and future would surely be intertwined to a limited (and healthier) extent.

The Future:
How Will We Watch Sports?

Times, they are a-changin'

JUST AS THE current state of affairs would have seemed like pure science fiction in the pre-Internet era, so will the current era of all-access, multilayered media appear antiquated someday. The first green shoots of a new media revolution are already visible. Some of these new technologies will go the way of passing fads, but others are bound to stay and mature until we will not be able to imagine consuming sports without them. Outlined in the following pages are some of the major developments in sports entertainment and technology:

Converging Live Game Experience and Social Media Presence
We have already seen glimpses of what the future of live spectator sports looks like. Any self-respecting new venue prides itself in the quality, size, and quantity of available cameras.

Aside from the obvious "pissing match"[14] factor, this modern-day stadium arms race hits upon a subtle flaw of modern day spectator sports.

Incorporating digital technology and social media to reinvent how fans interact and follow the game is the new frontier of the fan experience. One of the major players in this movement is the owner of the Sacramento Kings, Vivek Ranadive. Vivek's goal is *"to launch NBA 3.0."* (His words; evidently we are already living in the NBA 2.0 era.) The details are somewhat fuzzy, but according to Ranadive, *"We*

---

14 A contest of wills or egos, in this case among owners and stadium developers

have an opportunity to make basketball the premier sport of the twenty-first century...Kind of like what soccer was in the twentieth century. With technology you can expand social networks, you can give people an opportunity to participate and identify with it in ways that haven't been done before."[15]

Allow me to interject for a quick minute, Vivek. Being *"the sport of the twenty-first century"* will require much more than automatic Facebook check-ins, instant tweets, and Instagram posts with the touch of your thumb. The revenue-generating aspect of Mr. Ranadive's plan is much more robust. Part of the plan for the new arena includes calls for sending location-based offers such as team store merchandise sales, directly to the attending fans' mobile devices. In addition fans would be able to order concession stand items from their devices and have them delivered directly to their seats.

To help bring this new level of fan engagement to life, there are already broadcasting and technology companies looking to bring the coverage available during live games closer to the multi-layered, at-home experience. One of the major players in this field is Kiswe Mobile, a small outfit based in New Jersey. According to the company website, it promises to bring in a *"bevy of different video angles and vantage points, effectively adding a layer of depth to live sports events."* Kiswe would partner with the rights-owning networks in order to bring in viewing experiences combining the network's camera angles with Kiswe's own panoramic view cameras. Accessing this level of coverage would occur through the network's mobile application (your ESPN, NBC, or CBS sports app) without the fans knowing that a third party was behind the technology. This is what is referred to in digital media circles as a white label solution.

Essentially, both the objective and the presumed benefit consist of narrowing of the experiential gap between in-home access to sports entertainment and live, in-stadium viewing content. The spin being given by Kiswe is the "transformation of live events into mobile app

---

15 Riches, S. *"This Man Wants to Make the NBA a Social Network"*. Wired Magazine, December 2013.

experiences." Buzzwords and corpspeak aside, this begs the question of whether transforming a live event into an app experience is actually a good thing. In the end, you don't pay all this money on tickets to "transform" your experience into an app-viewing, couch-surfing event. That kind of action comes free and with a much better quality Wi-Fi feed.

Cynicism aside, I do see this as an inevitable step into the future. Arenas need to keep up with the vaster array of in-home coverage, otherwise they run the risk of hemorrhaging live attendance numbers and losing a piece of that sweet pie baked using the sports fans' disposable dough. "Smart Seats" are poised to become a necessity in any new area. The availability of in seat gadgets and entertainment may be restricted to premium seats at first but eventually we will come to consider a touch screen at our seats as much a part of our stadium experience as having a cup-holder at your seat.

At the same time, any blurring of the lines between live attendance and television viewing experience needs to be examined carefully. There is a reason fans choose to part with their disposable income to be a part of a live event, to be part of a larger-than-life experience. Does the ability to have enhanced social media content readily available while at the stadium contribute significantly to an enhanced spectator experience? Yes, it does, but to what degree or extent remains to be seen.

To quantify the impact of future developments in sports media, I'm including a Voiskow (as a nod to Maslow, but also as a token of respect to one of my bosses who kept mispronouncing my name, with "Voiskow" being one of his favorite ways to butcher the family name. It's "Voichescoo" dammit!) Hierarchy or Game-Changing Factor, in which 1 is the equivalent of going back to the rabbit-ears-antenna, black-and-white-TV days and 10 is a sure shot, stone cold guarantee, much like the likelihood that the sun shall rise again at dawn or that we will be using Internet in the near future.

As such, the multi-camera coverage during live games rating *(drumroll):*

Voiskow Game-Changing Factor (GCF): 7.
Offering spectators this type of live coverage during games needs to be a part of the future if attending live events is to maintain or grow its lure. The level of success hinges on the implementation details and actual content. While I believe that the multicamera access level needs to be commoditized (as we will see later), I can also see the integration of game footage as part of the live spectating experience as having minimal impact. As stated previously, I believe we are at the point of saturation when it comes to content. The focal point of a live game is and will continue to be the action unfolding live just a few steps away from your action-thirsty eyes. We attend live games to be a part of something greater than us, to bond with other fans during moments that transcend all demographics. Ultimately, both social media and game footage access are more easily available by *not* being live and in person at a game. Another factor working against this type of technology is the overreliance on a personal handheld device. If this were a more collective, group experience in which the fan base would partake in unique camera angles together I'd be more inclined to give it a higher grade on the Voiskow scale. However, the overreliance on a personal device, dependence on public Internet, and the stated goal of "transforming live events into mobile app experiences" has me hesitant. I cringe a little. We already have the mobile app experience. It takes place at home on our plush couch, with reliable Internet service and at no extra cost.

Sitting with me at the cynics' table, I also have a gentleman by the name of Mark Cuban, noted entrepreneur and owner of the Dallas Mavericks. According to Mr. Cuban *"The key for any NBA team is not falling into the lookdown trap...At the Mavs we want to entertain people enough during breaks that they forget to look at their phones. When people connect to their phones for anything other than an occasional text or e-mail, it means we have failed at entertaining our customers."*

While the perks of enhanced social media content availability are a natural step in the creation of a futuristic live game attendance experience, ultimately I believe that the fan sitting in the stands in person will look to maximize the emotions directly associated with being physically present at the game.

The #NextGen Craze—What Shall Ensue in Social Media?

Facebook, Twitter, Instagram, Snapchat, MySpace, Friendster. This rich stew of social media platforms has brought us closer, rendering physical distance (almost) irrelevant. Connecting with like-minded humans who share your interests and passions has never been easier.

But this is not the final frontier. Things are always in flux. Progress is the name of the game. Can't stop, won't stop.

What's #next then?

The Big Fish

Out of the usual social media suspects mentioned above, Facebook seems to be most aggressively courting the sports fan. Zuckerberg seems determined to put the *coq* in the social media *coq au vin*[16] dish. Cornering the "second screen market", which currently belongs to Twitter, the de facto medium to congregate and live blog/tweet your thoughts during the game, Facebook has created a hub aptly named the Facebook Sports Stadium. This is designed as a dedicated separate section of Facebook, split into four tabs, with each tab meant to serve all your secondary sports-watching needs. There is a tab for play-by-play details similar to ESPN's, a second tab where your friends'

---

16 A French dish of chicken braised with wine, lardoons, mushrooms, and (optionally) garlic. Related to the social media stew mentioned above.

comments are collated, a third tab with experts' comments—verified commentators, players, and other persons deemed bona fide sports personalities by Facebook, and a fourth and final tab with detailed stats.

Thus the jockeying for position continues. We know the role Twitter plays. It is very much part of the fabric of sports consumption, a de facto news wire, a (small) window into the soul of athletes, and a great source for punchy, in-game analysis and 140-character zingers.

Up until now, Facebook has been a place for postgame trash talk, as far as its impact on fans and fan culture is concerned. With the launch of the Stadium platform, Facebook is hoping to increase fan engagement *during* games by essentially replacing Twitter as the default second screen and creating a one-stop shop for all your secondary fandom needs. To what extent this proves successful will depend on the ability to create buzz and attract enough expert and pundit original content. As of the time of writing (May 2016), the "experts" section of Facebook Stadium consisted largely of updates from the social media accounts of the two teams playing the game in the virtual stadium.

In addition to off-the-cuff, shoot-from-the-hip original content, Twitter has the advantage of being first to market and locking in the early adopters. To a large extent, Twitter is better suited as a second screen, as it does not require a significant level of attention, thus allowing fans to continue devoting most of their attention to game action. The bare bones, simple timeline design is made up of snippets, quick updates, and the omnipresent #hottake.

No other tabs, no other distractions.

To what extent will Facebook be able to steal away eyeballs and attract a portion of the roar of the Twitter crowd during live events? It will depend on the success the company has luring fans to a more content-rich environment. The high-level numbers seem to favor Facebook—according to Facebook's own data, there are 650 million sports fans on its platform. Twitter, by contrast, has just 320 million monthly users in total.[17]

Snapchat is another major social media player that is looking for a piece of the pie. The constantly evolving social media app[18] features more than one hundred million daily users. Over the last two years, Snapchat has grown tremendously, overtaking Twitter in the much-coveted 18-to-34-year-old demographic in percentage of penetration within the segment as well as in the number of average monthly users.

Does this really capture the sports fans in the age demographic? Well, Snapchat is positioning itself to ensure that it does, as part of a clever approach to differentiate itself from the Twitter/Facebook stadium "timeline" experience.

Snapchat is providing a platform for stories and story telling, a crucial aspect of the limited-attention-span, short-lived news cycle we live in. These stories are disguised as ten-second video montages that create a more complete sensory experience for the user than a tweet and demand much less of an attention span than actually reading a more elaborate Facebook post does. The Snapchat content—the stories—are mostly user-generated content, as fans present at live events submit short videos (the story) of game action for contest entries. This type of fan involvement is a very effective method of increasing engagement and conveying a sense of belonging to the well-connected, social media–active fans, who also happen to be part of the much-coveted millennial demographics.

All the major US sports leagues have embraced Snapchat stories. According to Melissa Rosenthal, the NBA's senior vice president of digital media, *"Snapchat is a direct conduit into a highly engaged younger*

---

17 Lapowski, I. *"Facebook Takes on Twitter and ESPN with New Feature"*. Wired Magazine, January 2016.

18 Snapchat initially burst on the scene as a one-to-one ephemeral messaging app. Over the last three years, it has evolved into an avant-garde mobile media platform.

audience…as a proof point, half of our social media actions for tip-off came from Snapchat."[19]

As the content becomes richer, so do the demands on data usage. To avoid any potential impediment, leagues are subsidizing Wi-Fi improvements across all arenas, enabling fans to submit video content and encouraging this type of in-game engagement. In 2015 alone, MLB funded $300 million to bring better Wi-Fi service through a distributed antenna system in every major league stadium.

The other obvious candidate vying for a piece of sports social media pie is YouTube with its myriad of highlights and game-related content it spawns. By being a de facto video encyclopedia and a reference point for historical highlights ranging from Babe Ruth home runs, Wilt the Stilt highlights and the 1986 European Club Champions final penalty shootout, YouTube has changed the way we ingest sports content. Having the choice of watching live, yet mediocre content, versus feasting your eyes on incredible, era-defying highlight reels is a sports media game-changer. Quality matters. The "ooohs and aaahs" of watching say, Vince Carter dunk on Frederick Weiss are very real and the excitement hardly gets old even though the outcome is never in doubt[20].

Even beyond the highlights, The YouTube Generation has taken condensed content watching even further. As mentioned previously, there are millions of eyeballs focused on the emotion of sports as depicted through video reactions of fans watching their team succeed or fail. The merits of consuming this type of content are debatable but the draw to the next generation of fans is real. So real, in fact, that the CEO of BigBalls media, which owns Copa90, the YouTube channel focused mainly on fan reaction content, plans on taking on the behemoth of sports media, ESPN, and become the "undeniable home

---

19 Flynn, K. *"Sports On Snapchat: How 2015 Became The Year NBA, NFL, MLB, NHL Snapped Stories To Millennials"*. International Business Times, November 2015.

20 Arguably, the outcome was never in doubt just as Vince Carter was actually rising up for the Dunk over fifteen years ago, during the Sidney Olympics.

of youth football platform". This gentleman also believes *"the thing that has the scarcity and value – the broadcasting rights – is actually the thing that has the least value"*. Okay, then... I have to admit that it does indeed take big balls to claim that dudes watching other dudes watch sports is the way of the world and of the future.

However, stranger things have happened. Stay tuned and keep an open mind. "Old-school" sports fans and consumers better relish watching the NBA playoffs, the World Cup and the Super Bowl. Pretty soon we will be spending our time snapping and tweeting vines of random people watching these events. Oh, wait, we are already doing that.

Voiskow GCF: 10

There really isn't much up for debate or discussion here. The big social media whales are here to stay and will continue to swim along in the hyper-engaged, enriched-content, short-attention-span, instant gratification waters of sports seas.

The Small Fish

In addition to the giants of social media, smaller disrupters are bound to pop up looking for a piece of the action. Just as an example, there is a social media startup called Vixlet (hey now, that's a catchy name— part vixen, part starlet, 100 percent Vixlet) to create the world's first passion-based social network. According to Nick Loui, Vixlet's chief marketing officer, *"The next generation of social media will be about connecting you around passion. Sports are perfect, because you have people loving the team, the sport, and the league. It's truly global."*[21]

Sure, why not? The presumption is that the *current* generation of social media is really about connecting and keeping you in touch with friends and family, as well as providing a window into the soul of your favorite athletes and celebs, but it does not provide a deep enough

---

21 *Vixlet Uses Fan Passion to Create Next-Gen Social Networks.* Sport Techie, March 2016

reach when it comes to passions. I am not sure this is entirely accurate. Passions, hobbies, and interests are already engrained in the fabric of the modern social media. The emotional connections play a huge role in our social media lives. We engage based on hashtags, the lovechild of our passions, interests. This is why we already are #allin and belong to #bigblue, #patriotsnation (#ugh), and #ganggreen. #Wareagle.

Video content provided by Snapchat and largely endorsed by all major American sports leagues already has a deep visceral reach within the fans and fan bases. So allow me to set the bullshit meter on high when it comes to new apps on the social media scene that are essentially sugar coating the experience we are currently finding on established platforms and merely providing a nice, shiny wrap job on the structures already in place.

In the same pond of small to midsize players, we find the self-described "fastest growing sports social network," TOK.tv. The experiential features available through TOK.tv are delivered through a personalized interface that lets you interact and connect with other fans of the team you support. This presumes that you are a supporter of either Real Madrid, Barcelona, Juventus, or Serie A. Those are the only licensed partnerships at the moment. Aggressively touting the social aspect of fandom (*"You should never watch a match alone!"*) and courting the cord-cutting millennial (*"Who needs a TV anymore?"*), TOK.tv allows followers of the above-mentioned teams to talk (or "*tok*") to their fellow fans, cheer the goals, play stadium sounds and supporters' chants, and superimpose selfies over the game box score. Among the other aggressively marketed catchphrases is the promise that by cheering or booing, you are transporting yourself to the actual stadium. (*"Your friends will hear it. It will be like being all together at the Bernabeu!"*)

The red-blooded soccer hooligans and ultras of the '70s and '80s must be turning in their graves at the sounds and jingles of the smartphone-generated crowd noise, chants and booing. But, but...

this may just be where the modern experience of being a fan is headed. The social media hooligan has very different needs and outlets, and we must respect them in order to avoid being rooted in nostalgia.

Voiskow GCF: 6

It will be very tough for these small, niche players to break through. Yes, there may be a place for the barely legal Vixens, Starlets, and Tok-heads to sit at the kids' table and enjoy the bite-size candy, but in order to sit with the big boys and grab a large piece of the pie, they will require either massive bankrolls or truly game-changing capabilities in terms of feel, content, and experience.

The New Age of Live Sports
Humungous Screens, Stadium Perks, Suites, and Other Doodads

The days of concrete bowl stadiums where fans simply sat on wooden benches or stood in terraces and stared, fixated, at the field, deprived of any other form of entertainment are long gone. Today's game-day experience would probably make many a sunflower-seed-chewing fan from the '60s lose his damn mind. There are stadium-specific apps and Wi-Fi access that allow for a range of possibilities, stretching from ordering food from your seat to checking out the duration of the restroom facilities line, with a social media check in between. With all these exciting possibilities in the palm of their hands, is it really shocking that fans spend most of their time at the stadium staring at their screens?

As one of the last live, in-the-moment events in a fragmented and decentralized media world, the live game experience faces a lot more competition. Technology has made it easy and convenient for fans to engage with a sporting event on their own terms, in their own space. Becoming disengaged from a live event is becoming the norm, rather than the exception. A Cisco study from 2012[22] found that *57 percent of sports fans prefer watching the game at home.* In addition, research from sports demographer Rich Luker suggests millennials won't automatically fill seats vacated by their parents: the greatest decline in avid sports fans in the last decade has come among 12- to 17-year-olds and 18- to 34-year-olds.[23]

My Screen Size Brings All the Boys to the Yard

As television feed quality has gotten megapixelated, offering crystal clear quality, it has also leveraged another tool at its disposal: multi-layered content (fantasy stats, headlines, replays) and multi-angle camera views. As a television viewer, you now have the ability to take in the action from multiple angles, gaining an in-depth understanding of the game action from multiple vantage points. In addition, broadcasters are emphasizing specific, often times subtler aspects of the game that may have gone unnoticed in the early days of TV broadcasting. Being at home, you have the ability to consume whatever game-related content you choose to by checking out highlights and replays on social media or on your television, as well as keeping up with your fantasy team performance, all at the same time.

You also have the comfort, the replays, the multi-camera angles, and the highlights. Why would anyone deal with traffic, crowds, expensive concession stands, and unwieldy fans when they could consume a game on their own terms, with arguably better tools at their disposal, allowing them to relish the action in a complete and complex manner.

Although the live game atmosphere continues to be unique, in the sense that it brings fans closest to the action and allows them to publicly support their teams, the factors above need to be

---

22 "The Connected Sports Fan". *Insights from the Cisco IBSG Horizons Study.* September 2012.

23 Mickle, T. *"Industry looks for right recipe to attract fans among millennials".* Sports Business Daily, March 2014.

addressed. The modern stadium developers and franchise owners are facing continuing pressure on the design side to create venues that are more flexible and more amazing and can one-up what the fans can get at home.

Currently, the arms race among owners financing and building new stadiums is aimed at creating bigger and better screens. The line in the sand has been drawn. It is Jerry Jones monstrosity at AT&T Field, which measures 160 feet wide and 72 feet high, for about 40,000 square feet of LED, if we include all four panels. The Atlanta Falcons' new stadium is set to one-up this with an even bigger screen: a circular video board intended to surround a large part of the stadium in a LED display, 58 feet high and 1,100 feet wide, for a whopping 64,000 square feet of LED display. In other words, the sure way to get ahead of this screen size dick-measuring contest is to surround the whole damn stadium with a screen. More than that, the new Atlanta stadium will also feature 20,000 square feet of additional LED boards, ensuring that fans have the opportunity to keep up with the fantasy game stats, replays, and highlights that are usually available at home.

It's basically a case of "if you can't beat them, join them." In other words, in the live event versus TV/tablet screen fight for eyeballs and engagement, the stadium designers and investors are conceding that it is indeed screens people want[24], so screens they will give them. Call it "synergy" and put a bow on it. Toggling between different screens appears to be the way of the future, whether at home or in live attendance.

Smart Seats, Sweet Suites, and the Unbearable Lightness of Being a Spectator

As discussed in the pages above, watching sports has become all about the communal experience. Perhaps *"Take me out to the ballgame, take me*

---

24 Total screen time per capita, including television, had increased 8% between 2013 and 2014, according to a Nielsen Study

out with the crowd" has always been the modus operandi of the spectator; only now, it seems the modern fan seeks to recreate an experience
closer to that of watching the game at home or at a bar. Being with and
interacting with your friends during the game is a quintessential part
of the whole live stadium fan experience. It seems that at every game I
attend, a vast majority of fans spend a lot more time *not* watching the
game than actually watching and being engaged in the live action. The
not-watching-the-game-while-at-the-game trend is becoming more
widespread as the seats get better or more expensive. This is not sur-
prising, since most of the extracurricular perks are targeted directly
at the moneyed crowd, whose attention and wallets the stadium and
franchise owners are overtly targeting. These are the social butterfly
fans, the "see and be seen" crowd, who are essentially using the game
as a pretext to gather around, socialize, and network. Frankly, I place
no blame on them for being distracted. With so much going on around
them, they would have to be some misplaced, anachronistic fans, firmly
planted in their romantic idealist roots, to have any hope of having an
unadulterated focus on the live-game action. The days of sitting, staring at the field, and mumbling through sunflower seeds are over.

The reality is that the modern live-game watching experience is
directly aimed at the high tech, gadgets, and perks fan base, which is
generally more concerned with the social aspects of being a spectator
than with the athletic prowess or spectacle on the field.

Smart Seats are becoming the gadget *du jour* when it comes to
enhancing and modernizing the live spectator experience. A touch
screen with multiple capabilities ranging from streaming video to
social media connectivity and in-game stats firmly places the spectator in an ecosystem of hardware, applications, and software, providing a rich visual experience directly from the stadium seat. Initially
a must-have contraption of the well-heeled luxury suites and front
row sections, the smart seat is becoming more prevalent with new
some stadiums including it as a standard feature (latest example is
the Docklands Stadium in Melbourne).

For the sake of nuance and accuracy, it bares mentioning that the degree to which the spectator is distracted from the game varies by sport. Heading over for some old-timey baseball at the park? Hope you do your research beforehand on places to meet, where to have your beers, and where to go for dessert. Basketball? Dancers, DJs, and T-shirt cannons will keep the party going; just make sure you have a good exit system allowing you to access that barbecue spot where the brisket is always moist, and you time your meal time properly avoiding the crowds (usually the beginning of the second quarter is what you should aim for[25]).

On the other hand, if you are at a hockey game or soccer game, you might want to just pay attention. Both are inherently great live sports that require constant attention. Great plays happen without any foreplay or warning. The likelihood that you could end up missing *THE* highlight of the game is strong enough to deter you from wandering the corridors searching for Gummy Bears and Cracker Jacks during game action. There are fewer timeouts and less in the way of nongame spectacle taking place on the ice or field.

You want another cool feature of the next gen stadia? How about line-shortening technology? That's right, the WaitTime app is already here to ensure that your precious time at the ballpark is optimized. WaitTime uses "patent-pending crowd-science technology [that] provides real-time information on fan traffic to major entertainment and sports venues" and does so in an effort to ultimately eliminate the majority of long lines to get food or go to the bathroom at all venues—not just athletic ones.

Count me in.

Voiskow GCF: 9

Whether we like it or not, changes are coming. This is another subject that is not really up for debate, just a matter of staying tuned and

---

25 I promise this is the extent of any instructions on "how to watch sports"

flexible to the evolution of live sports. The era of the new stadiums is coming, and it will continue to shape the way we watch live sports and attend games. There is enough empirical evidence in the way of both existing and upcoming stadium perks, thus allowing us to eliminate any room for debate. The extent to which any given fan will be connected to social media while at the stadium is dependent upon the type of fan and person he/she happens to be. The technology to keep us connected to our virtual networks while at the new arenas is already here or being implemented.

No, it is extremely unlikely that we will see a return to the day of the concrete dome stadium, devoid of the huge-ass screens, the social media integration, and pulled pork and craft beer concession stands.

I believe in the future. I believe in progress. Go ahead and order another craft brew; odds are you won't have to wait that long for the bathroom. There's an app for that.

Virtual Reality

Futures made of virtual insanity now
Always seem to, be govern'd by this love we have
For useless, twisting, our new technology…

(*JAMIROQUAI, 1996*)

O NE OF THE dominant buzzwords coming out of the 2016 Consumer Electronics Show is Virtual Reality (VR). Once again, the sports world appears to be leading the way with content delivery to VR sets. NBA media appears committed to the VR channels and the afferent race to bring content to market as part of the next big thing in media. The NBA has broadcast games to virtual reality headsets, and none other than the King, LeBron James, recently starred in his own immersive film. Certainly, the idea of being submerged in a virtual world where you have the sense of taking part in a star athlete's life is extremely appealing.

On October 27, 2015, the NBA became the first major sports league to offer live-streaming game action in virtual reality. During the opening-night matchup between the Golden State Warriors and New Orleans Pelicans in Oakland, California, the league provided fans a view of the contest in its entirety from the perspective of courtside-seated fan. The virtual reality stream used in last October's Warriors-Pelicans game allowed viewers to focus their attention anywhere in arena, a full 360 degrees, at any time. In an attempt to replicate the experience of actually being at a game, there was no commentary, only crowd and court noises.

We can eliminate shortage of content from the list of challenges facing the VR industry. Just this April, the NCAA and its broadcast partners live streamed the Men's Final Four semifinals and the title game in virtual reality. The list should continue to grow over time. In the future, as the practice of streaming games in virtual reality becomes more common, many in the industry expect each broadcast to feature a handful of cameras, capturing unique angles that can be cycled through at the control of the user.

In conjunction with multiple cameras, NextVR, one of the company behind this revolutionary technology, uses 3-D audio. In essence 3-D audio is the next-level, surround-sound experience. What sets it apart is the ability to allow the user to determine his or her audio experience, dependent on the location of their attention focus. For example, if the action during an NBA game is happening at one end of the court, face the opposite direction, and the sound of squeaking shoes and shouting players will diminish. The result is a truly immersive spatial reality that tricks the brain into believing you are in the middle of the action.

NextVR's vision of the future spectator is aggressively futuristic. The company sees a future in which even haptic[26] feedback is included. Intel's RealSense Interaction Design Group is currently developing a system that would take information gathered from three-dimensional camera rigs like those used by NextVR and turn it into vibrations across a number of sensors woven into clothing worn by the viewer. In plain English, the goal is not only to make what you feel and hear feel completely lifelike, but also to bring the feel of being in the arena to wherever VR technology exists. The pulsating reverberations of the in-house PA system, the whooshing feeling of

---

26 Haptic (adj.): Of or relating to the sense of touch, in particular relating to the perception and manipulation of objects using the senses of touch and proprioception.

players running past you, and the piercing roar of the crowd could be felt remotely the way they are (currently) only felt when you are attending a game in person.

Brad Allen, the executive chairman of NextVR, has spoken of a future in which users can trigger the display of social media feeds using head gestures or by simply turning 180 degrees to view a social hub directly behind them during games. Mr. Allen even sees a future in which users can interact with these feeds and post content themselves entirely through the device. And in an even more distant, but likely not-too-distant future, he imagines headsets that allow viewers to mesh whatever they're watching with a view of what's immediately around them outside of their VR experience.

The future game-watching experience may be just as immersive whether we are in our seat at the stadium or at home on the couch.

Voiskow GCF: 8

The experiential aspect of VR should continue to benefit from the increasing content, giving fans more access to their sports idols' world.

Examining VR technology strictly from the vantage point of its impact on the game-watching experience, it is evident there are some kinks left to sort out before VR content can be considered truly game-changing. Scalability appears to be an issue, with demand for VR sets apparently slacking; with only about two million HMDs (head-mounted display) sets on the global market today and with a fore-casted penetration of only 8% by 2018. To put that in perspective, the penetration rate of pay TV (television-owning households paying for TV service out of total US households) is a gigantic 81%. Worth notic-ing is that the pay TV rate has gone down from 87 percent in 2010, although compared to a decade ago (77% in 2005), it is up.

However, the most significant challenge facing large-scale VR dis-tribution is a technical one. As of early 2016, VR technology is not capable of adjusting for depth and distance at the individual camera level. The setting of the camera capturing VR content is fixed; there is no dynamic change to position, orientation, or field of view. The same focal point is shown, with a predetermined set of views.

In essence, this limitation prevents VR technology from bringing a true front-row-access type of experience. Absent the ability to focus and depth perception, the wide-angle shot is limited compared to the television feed or the human eye.

Part of Mr. Allen's vision is eerily reminiscent of tech fads that never quite panned out as game changers: "*A future in which users can trigger the display of social media feeds using head gestures or by simply turning 180 degrees to view a social hub directly behind them during games*". That sounds a bit too much like a reincarnation of the Google Glass. You do not want to be associated with any device that has been knows as "Glasshole" or "Bluedouche". Google Glass was a huge bust for a laundry list of reasons.[27]

If the stagnant evolution of VR headsets (HMDs) and the Google Glass combustion are telling us anything, it is that, for the most part, we as humans are hesitant to don a piece of head or eye gear in order to alter our immediate reality. We are content pulling our smart screens out of our pockets at a time of our choosing or staring at them on our wrists, but having a piece of hardware completely attached to our heads and affixed directly in front of our eyesight crosses the breaking point of interference with a basic way of going through life. It limits our basic human condition and the means through which we experience life.

For all its shortcomings related to live game consumption, it is worth mentioning that VR is having a tremendous impact on modern training. Teams and athletes use VR in order to recreate game conditions and events. Companies like EON Sports take live game

---

27 Google Glass has been put on hold. Here is a glorious passage from Wired's review of the device: "*Glass is socially awkward. Again and again, I made people very uncomfortable. That made me very uncomfortable. People get angry at Glass. They get angry at you for wearing Glass. They talk about you openly. It inspires the most aggressive of passive aggression. Bill Wasik refers apologetically to the Bluedouche principle. But nobody apologizes in real life. They just call you an asshole.*"
Honan, M. "*I, Glasshole: My Year With Google Glass*". Wired Magazine, December 2013.

data and provide immersive game-like conditions through computer generated graphics broadcast in the HMD, thus enabling athletes to prepare for their next opponent. Notably, athletes such as Jameis Winston and Carson Palmer have been known to train using VR technology. This is game-film preparation taken to the next level, with conclusive training benefits. Both athletes enjoyed tremendous success in the post-period of the VR experiment.

Augmented Reality

First off, what exactly is this Augmented Reality (or AR) you speak of, Mr. Voiskow?

The short answer is that Augmented Reality is a visual or audio overlay on real content, live or on delay, being broadcast on a screen. To a large degree Augmented Reality is already here. Think of the yellow first down markers shown during football games or game analysts highlighting areas of play on the screen such as: offside lines, formations, and strike zones to help the viewers gain a better understanding of certain aspects of the game. These are the current applications of AR, a key part of our viewing experience for over a decade.

Also, let's not forget the infamous FoxTrax or Glow Puck, developed in the late '90s to help viewers follow the puck on their pre-HD screens. Canadian hockey buffs are still laughing about it. As ridiculed as the glowing puck ended up being, the yellow-red dot with a trailing comet tail is a prime example of what AR is at its core.

Superimposed data used to enhance the user experience is becoming a key part of being a spectator, whether at home in front of the screen or at the game. For the most part, AR technology has been used to enhance game broadcasting with additional information and game nuance, ultimately enabling the fans to gain a deeper understanding of live game action. In addition, we have seen a proliferation of news tickers, score bars and others somewhat invasive graphics that aim to give us information about other games, events, or breaking news. The rise of fantasy sports has given impetus to another layer of screen data and screen space during live games.

Voiskow GCF: 7

If I had had to rate this topic five years ago, the grade would have been a point or so higher. Nowadays, there is a sense that we have reached a breaking point at which additional screen data or game-broadcast augmentation has gone way past helpful and useful, inched past invasive and is nearing the intrusive. We are seeing a movement toward simplification and clarity of in-game graphics, toward a cleaner, crisper screen. Witness the recent screen cleanup implemented by NBC Sports for its English Premier League game broadcasting. Smaller and more transparent box score, limited to no in-game ads or distractions, a commitment to dedicating a greater portion of the screen to the game than prior broadcasts.

It is worth noting that this movement toward in-game simplification has coincided with the rise in social media. In the age of Twitter and Facebook, fans prefer to augment their game-watching experience by self-sourcing their information and data individually through social media, rather than being force fed information by the networks. We want our game footage to be just that, without any distractions.

We may continue to see an increase in screen "noise" during pre-, post-, and halftime shows. Essentially, this is the time when the broadcast networks get to flex their graphic design muscles, put on a futuristic feel, and make up for all that lost screen time during the live action. ESPN's SportsCenter, the poster child for sporting news, has gone through a recent revamp. Although the amount of data and information presented on the screen has not been reduced, the new feel follows the same trends as live game broadcasting. It is sharper and cleaner, with brighter fonts and team logos and a smoother scroll, perhaps even taking some inspiration from recent Apple products.

As far as live, in-stadium game watching goes, we may still be in the early stages of AR implementation. Currently, there are some work-in-progress smartphone capabilities that would allow fans to aim their devices toward a player and, through use of image recognition, receive information about that player, superimposed on their smartphones. These capabilities are still being developed at the individual stadium, sport, and player level. However, as early as 2009, at the Wimbledon tennis tournament, the Wimbledon Seer app was introduced. It was developed by IBM, and ran on Google's Android smart phone. The user looks through the phone's camera lens and receives superimposed data on various aspects of the Wimbledon experience. That data included match information, a news feed, a locator function, and even refreshment stand updates.

"Your Call" and the Future of Broadcasting

Broken down, a live game broadcast is made up of two basic elements: a live video feed and an audio feed. Up until a few years ago, the quest for the perfect game broadcast was focused on the quality of the video feed. The broadcast networks began investing in video caption and transmittal equipment that would add pixels and enable the consumer to enjoy ever-higher levels of image resolution.

The other part, the audio, was more of a given, in the sense that anyone with a surround sound high fidelity system in their home was able to create an exceptional game-watching ambiance. Networks started introducing various "sounds of the game" gimmicks, such as replays of the ball making contact with the bat, live unedited shots from the team huddles, and the back-of-the-neck-hair-raising sounds of thousands of fans chanting in the stadium. It became a fairly simple formula: bring in high-resolution image content and lots of it, add in some live, in-stadium sound bites to replicate the live watching experience, and *voila*—you have one high-quality, high-fidelity, engaging broadcast.

Recently, some enterprising "disrupters" realized that there is a layer of customization that could actually make the game-watching experience even more personalized. While the video feed is set and not subject to any changes (the game is the game is the game), the audio commentary can take on many shapes and feels. There doesn't have to be just one audio feed that millions of fans need be subjected to. We don't all have to grumble and moan on Twitter about the play-by-play announcer missing a key detail or mixing up some players or just generally coming off as a blithering idiot. It doesn't have to be this way.

The next generation of audio commentary could be sourced from user-generated content and allow the audience to select among a number of individualized feeds provided by freelance commentators. Fans have started relying on specialized blogs and digital media for their daily consumption of team coverage. Below are a few data points[28] to back up this claim:

- *Between 2011 and 2013, we saw a 67% increase in the number of fans who engage in social media as part of their live sports consumption routine.*
- *For the same time period, there was a 13% increase in general online sports consumption (measured by screen time minutes) and a 65% increase in sports consumption through mobile devices.*
- *During the same time period, television and print media consumption were down 2.5% and 2%. These media channels are usually representative of the one-size fits all, national coverage.*

Blanketed, one-size-fits-all local newspaper coverage is not sufficient any more. We want to hear different voices and points of view that provide the kind of angles and nuances that make sports more interesting. As fans are seeking out a more personalized, unique perspective, this rising tide of accompanying content should ultimately be able to lift all boats, including those that are starting to specialize in play-by-play and color commentary.

At time of print, a small outfit dubbed *yourcall.tv* markets itself to the fans seeking a more personal, customized audio feed by asking whether "*you mute the announcers during sporting events? Are you tired*

---

28 *Stadd, A.* "More Sports Fans Turning To Digital Media Over TV". *AdWeek, August 2013.*

of biased sportscasters? Think you and your friends could do a better job?"[29]
This type of pitch presumably addresses the growing trend of sports
watching as an a la carte, on-your-own-terms experience, as opposed
to the traditional one-size-fits-all coverage. When you have the ability
to follow your own personalized voices on social media, it is only a
matter of time before you, as the fan at large, have the ability to listen
to the actual voices commentating during a live game.

Voiskow GCF: 7.5

Whether it is a small outfit like yourcall.tv or one of the bigger players
in streaming media, such as *Twitch*, the fundamental shift to customized audio is coming. This development could potentially create a
market of sports announcers with the ability to create a following or
capitalize on an already-existing following in order to draw a high
volume of eardrums and begin monetizing this type of skill and service. Think of the all the influencers and "tastemakers" on Twitter
with a large following. Now picture them with microphone in front of
them, giving you a feel for the game similar to the tone of their commentary through their tweets. Clearly relating live play-by-play action
is a different skill set requiring much more exertion than sending out
140-character blurbs.

The major hesitation I have stems from the isolationist impact that
customized commentary might have. Part of the unifying aspect of
sports comes from the way fans complain, quip and clown[30] the same
commentary inadequacies that we all hear. Part of the fabric that
threads our fandom experience together is made up of the generic,
national-scale commentary that *all of us* listen to. There is comfort
in the fact that a blunder in the play-by-play announcing or a not-so-
subtle bias in commentary is heard by us all. We've come to find a
certain level of comfort from the imperfections and idiosyncrasies we

---

29 https://www.yourcall.tv/how-it-works.html
30 clown, as in *make fun of*

associate with each talking head. We have an arsenal of jokes ready to be deployed whenever a commentator slips up in expected fashion. This allows us to connect with one another and share the same bonding fan experience. What would happen to all our social media mockery and banter if we went our separate ways in search of personalized commentary? How would we be able to come together and relate to all the crying Jordan memes?

Stretching the argument to its limits, if a brilliant yourcall.tv commentator mixes up his metaphors (after all, no one is perfect), does that add anything to the general fans' discourse? If a tree falls in the forest and no one hears it, does it make a sound? The great thing about social media is that society at large is able to convene in one virtual space in order to comment and whine about current, shared events happening on a grand scale. On the other hand, a fragmented type of fan experience, in which small segments of fans begin creating our own microcosms by constructing and delighting in our own, personalized type of consumption would forbid this type of coming together. Ultimately, this ability to partake in a common experience goes right to the core of fandom. Bitching and moaning about communal subjects is a significant aspect of fandom. Give us fewer things to grumble about, and we feel less fulfilled. The entire fan experience is rendered less complete.

As noteworthy a technological advancement as customized, personalized broadcasting is, it will probably not be a paradigm shifter. With all the flaws and biases (and there are many), the ladies and the gentlemen who comment on the action put in significant time and preparation that the vast majority of amateur play-by-play callers just don't have. Imperfect as color commentators and play-by-play announcers are, there is a reason why they are paid to do this.

To be clear, there is a place for custom broadcasting. For the budding announcer and the articulate and passionate fan, this type of medium is most welcomed. However, it is hard to see it going beyond the fringes of sports culture and into the popular discourse.

Drones, Nixies, GoPros, and Cons

IN THE YEAR of the Lord 2016, it is becoming increasingly difficult to be successful in any field without constant efforts of self-promotion. Personal "brand" and "image" are part of the everyday vocabulary in the modern era of self-aggrandizement and narcissism applied through social media. This general attitude has seeped over to the sporting world. There are only a handful of athletes in every sport whose performance, metrics, and highlights speak for themselves. A few rungs down the pole of any sport there is an ever-increasing segment of athletes who need to stand out and become marketable through a higher level of notoriety. They have something to prove, they need to stand out. Luckily for them, there are a slew of technological advancements that essentially eliminate the need for a personal cameraman to capture the highlights and low-lights of a young athlete. Drone-like devices are now able to satisfy an increasing demand by bringing a unique perspective to content and performance that is just below the cusp of extraordinary. As exciting as it would be to capture all-star athletes midflight as they throw down the rock, or make a spectacular catch, the athletes who stand to benefit immediately are the ones who are looking to get noticed, looking for a breakthrough, or dreaming of ending up on *SportsCenter Top 10.*

As video-capture devices become more and more prevalent, we, the fans, will be exposed to the point of saturation with backyard, playground, and street ball highlights of great athletes who fall just below the line of being household names.

Up until 2013–2014, technology allowed for body camera installations that would capture firsthand content from the vantage of the athlete. This made for great material to feed their followers, fans, and other social media acolytes. YouTube still has terabytes of video featuring amped-up, overcaffeinated dudes jumping off cliffs, shredding waist deep snow, or swimming with sharks. No self-respecting boarder, surfer, or biker neglected to mount the GoPro prior to embarking on a potentially bone-crushing ride. Video or it never happened.

The adrenalin-inducing footage was originally directed at the "Do the Dew," Red Bull–guzzling, X Games generation, and the extreme, individual sports market. The merits of GoPro are undeniable. Those videos are...*fun*. And that's about it. Not that fun isn't enough, but the market was and still is evolving both from the consumer's and the content creator's standpoint. The next wave of video self-capture has been taking the game beyond just fun. The drone-like technology that has emerged in the teen years of the new millennium enables a larger segment of athletes to promote their abilities, to develop a brand and a larger social media presence, and ultimately gain greater exposure to recruiters and agents.

OK, Voiskow, that's cool and all, but does this impact me, the fan, at all?

Voiskow GCF: 6

Short answer is that footage from drone-like cameras doesn't impact you a whole lot unless you happen to follow athletes and events on the fringe or are into X-Games athletes. Across the different archetypes of major professional league fans, this would probably not register in terms of sports consumption habits. However, if you are into college sports, minor leagues, and extreme sports, the drone-like technology provides major advantages. The fact that a seventeen-year-old kid can throw a quadcopter equipped with a camera in the air and throw down a 360-degree dunk, summersault into the end zone, and make a one-handed catch will get you lusting for more and salivating at the prospect of having such a talented young individual wearing your team's colors.

The footage quality coming from a Nixie is nothing short of spectacular. You get an aerial, full-1080p HD view of the action.

Backing up a step, it would be fantastic to see highlights of your bona fide superstars provided from an above-the-rim, personal drone camera. Who wouldn't want to watch LeBron or Russ Westbrook put on a slam-dunk recital of sorts from the unique perspective afforded by aerial drone cameras? Or be able to watch eye-popping catches from Odell Beckham Jr. on a regular basis from the comfort of their home?

The reality is that there is very limited upside in this type of technology for the true stars of the game. Guys earning eight figures a year don't need to prove anything from an athletic prowess standpoint. Unless they are contractually obligated to do so, there is no real benefit to providing this type of behind-the-scenes, personalized content to the world.

So yes, the Nixie is a great gadget...but that's about it. Once you've seen a few adrenaline-fueled aerial highlights, you have seen them all.

eSports

eSports? Are we really going to start watching dudes play shoot-'em-up video games on their Nintendo? Yes. Yes, we are. Maybe not you and I, but millions of other "sports fans" will.

The question above was probably asked by some pundit (or literary debutante) concerned about the TV viewership of a program showing dudes playing cards. Enter the *hole cam*. Once the hole cam burst on the scene, the audience for poker on TV skyrocketed. Let's get our mind right - to avoid any confusion - the *hole cam* refers to the type of camera that allows TV poker audiences to see the hidden cards that players hold. The aforementioned hole cam, along with the live-sports feel provided by amped-up commentators, overly agitated about queens and kings in the hole, the crisp graphics and the general excitement that comes along with live contests contributed to the booming popularity of the "sport."

People watch this stuff. There are actual humans tuning in to ESPN to watch professional athletes (!) play video games against one another. As evidenced by the chart below, the biggest eSports tournaments (*League of Legends*) rival any sporting event in terms of viewership.

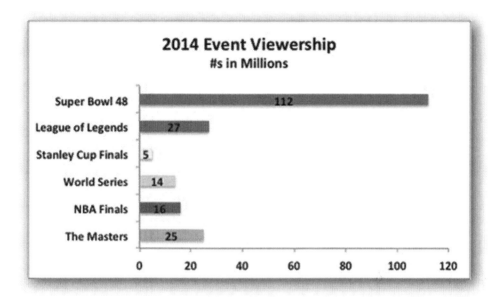

To give more context regarding the magnitude of eSports: Some 205 million people watched or played eSports in 2014, according to market research firm *Newzoo*. And while eSports have had the strongest following in Asia, especially in gaming-mad Korea, North America and Europe now claim twenty-eight million eSports fans, and the number is growing by 21 percent a year.

Twitch, a video-streaming site that boasts a hundred million unique visitors per month, is arguably the most important contributor to eSports' recent growth. Offering streams of games and tournaments and access to gaming's stars, it is also the place where the next generation of gamers can post their own streams. And evidently, someone is watching. Even if you are not familiar with *Twitch*, you definitely heard about this little website called YouTube. Keeping a pulse on the number of followers by category, we can form a good idea of the magnitude of impact and influence that eGames hold in today's sports and entertainment world.[31]

---

31 *YouTube follower data from Casselman, Ben.* "Resistance is futile: eSports is massive... and growing". *ESPN, The Magazine, June 2015.*

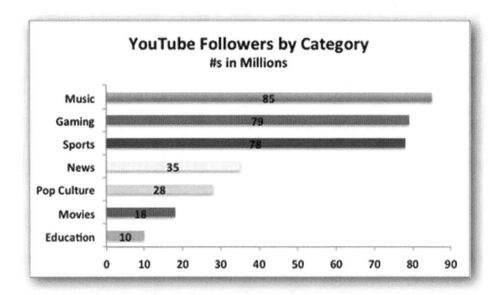

Let's back up a minute. What exactly are eSports?

The eSports content is made up of your usual suspects, the most popular video games across the spectrum of genres: a classic shooter *Call of Duty: Ghosts*; a strategy game *Starcraft II: Heart of the Swarm*; and some fighting games for good measure—*Super Smash Brothers Melee, Injustice: Gods Among Us,* and *Killer Instinct.*

The latest development in the line of eGames broadcasting involves Formula E, the electric car version of Formula 1 racing. Touting multicamera feeds from driver perspective and a "number of virtual camera locations and audio of the race," the Formula E brass is looking to offer an eGames-like experience to viewers in this market, with the slight twist that in this case the action on the screen is a rendition of an actual live event, featuring real cars and real human pilots, as opposed to a video game.

Voiskow GCF: 8.5

Look, I am not saying that eSports represent the Future of Sports (or The Truth). But we simply cannot deny the data. The numbers are astounding. People tune in to this. Ball don't lie. More people watched League of Legends in 2014 than the NBA finals. There is a significant underground culture of eSports fans that exists outside the fringes of traditional mainstream sports. eSports may not replace any of the major sports, but it's evident that substantial numbers of followers tune in across the globe, justifying the consideration of eSports as part of the general sporting discourse.

As old-timey sports like horse racing[32] and boxing ride into the sunset, we will continue to see the rise of games, contests, and activities better suited for the digital age. This shift to eGames also speaks to the democratization of sport and the greater amount of time devoted to screens. Any kid with a console and a dream can be a star. That hope and that level of accessibility enable a higher level of fandom and following. For the vast majority of kids, it becomes much more difficult to visualize being a triple crown jockey winner or even a major leaguer than to envision winning a part of the prize money at one of the eGames tourneys. Being able to hone your craft in your own basement while playing a game with an extremely low entry cost becomes a much more attractive scenario versus spending thousands of hours grinding, sweating, and getting beat up. Why would anyone prefer riding a horse or getting punched in the nose when you could train and dream big right there in your mama's basement? Sky's the limit.

While rumors of millennials being soft might be greatly exaggerated, millions of young ones across the globe are not running any risk of being aggressed (micro or otherwise...) while playing video games. Safety first, safety last and safety in between. Let us adjourn here in a safe space.

---

32 2015 was a big year for horse racing. We had our first Triple Crown winner in 37 years. Even so, attendance and TV ratings continue to decline to historic lows.

October 22, 2017

Action!

A Savant, a Contrarian and a Utilitarian walk into a bar. A Social Butterfly and a Romantic Loyalist, along with a dozen flat-screens and blaring pop music greet them.

"Oh, great, they're already down a touchdown. Told y'all this team ain't going nowhere...I'll be in that booth on my Oculus Rift. Holler at me when you're done". The Contrarian puffs his chest and straps on the VR headset, ensuring everyone takes notice.

"Well, actually, they have the third-best winning percentage in the league coming back from 10 points or less, so this is not over by any means, fellas." The Savant pulls up his phone and furiously tweets this very same phrase.

"Well, I took them at + 9 so as long as they can keep it a one score game I'm good. Also, I have Johnson on my fantasy team and he's put up a ton of yards already." The Utilitarian sits down and giddily pulls up her tablet to check her fantasy team stats.

"Ohhh, check her out...little shorty with the Bears hat." The Social Butterfly walks over lifting a pint glass and giving an awkward *"Da Bears!"* toast in his best Ditka voice. The Bears fan doesn't bite just yet. The Butterfly has found a team to root for.

"Trying to watch the game here guys, let's save all that sweet talk for later, eh?...Hey buddy, I'll have another round". The Romantic stares blankly. Can't even watch a ballgame anymore. To make matters worse, there is a group of college kids sitting in a booth who look like they are

playing video games. This is what happens when you give free wifi. No interest in the actual game, damn shame..."Da Bears!"...Oh wait, are they actually *watching* video game footage? Is this for real?

For real indeed. This is how we do it.

Game Over.

THE END

Acknowledgements

M OST APPRECIATIVE TO Andrea and Benji, without whose love and support this book would not exist.

A special thank you to those whose input and guidance are the only reasons why you may have found parts of the book that you actually enjoyed: Mike Quinn, Sam Sneed, Ryan Sengara, Dan Dundara, Brad Rothschild, Linda "Freedaghetto", Alex Coman, Alex Torres, Tom Helleberg.

A massive hug and all the love to my parents, Virgil and Sanda. They kept the lights and the cable on and put up with my nonsense even when I became way too vested in watching 22 men chase a round object on the screen for my own good.

Thank you to the Whole Foods at Columbus Circle, could not have done this without your morning brews and free wifi.

And dedicated to America, whatever that is.

About the Illustrator

MANY THANKS TO Rigo Pinto, who helped bring the fan archetypes to life through the cover art and illustrations.

Rigo has been highly influenced and inspired by Walt Disney from an early age. Intrigued by all things in the entertainment world, Rigo worked in the radio industry while studying art and developing his drawing skills at Pasadena City College. He then transferred to the ArtCenter College of Design in Pasadena to pursue his degree in Illustration Entertainment with a focus on Character Design. With a year left before graduation, he is now focused on preparing his portfolio and perfecting his skills. Rigo's goal is to work for the Walt Disney Company or Pixar so he can continue touching people's hearts through the art of animation.

Instagram: @RigoPintoJr
Twitter: @RigoPintoJr

Made in the USA
San Bernardino, CA
16 July 2016